Travel Guide To
ISRAEL

Robert Lindsted

Hearthstone Publishing Ltd.
P.O. Box 815 · Oklahoma City, Ok 73101

A Division Of
Southwest Radio Church Of The Air

ISBN 0-9624517-5-4

Table of Contents

Title	Page

Israel
  The Holy Land 2
  Map — Israel 5
  General Information........................ 6
  Map — Land of the Gospels: Economical... 11
  Map — Land of the Gospels:
     Travel Routes.......................... 12
  Israeli Agriculture 13
  Summary of Modern Israeli History 16
  Outline of Israel's History 18

Geographical Area
  Map — Land of the Gospels:
     Topographical 22
  Topography of Israel 23
  Map — The Land of Israel: East to West ... 26
  Map — The Land of Israel:
     North to South 27
  Galilee 28
  Plain of Esdraelon........................... 34
  Samaria 36
  Ha-Negeb.................................... 46

Wilderness of Judea 48
Jordan River 49
Sea of Galilee.............................. 55
Biblical Cities
Acre 63
Beersheba................................... 64
Bethlehem 65
Map — Bethlehem 70
Caesarea.................................... 71
Capernaum 75
Jericho 79
Jerusalem................................... 85
Map — Solomon's Temple 105
Map — Jerusalem and Vicinity 106
Map — Jerusalem, West Old City 107
Map — Jerusalem, East Old City 108
*Map — Crucifixion Week of Christ in
    Jerusalem* 109
Joppa-Tel Aviv 110
Masada..................................... 113
Map — Masada 119
Megiddo.................................... 120
Nazareth................................... 122
Samaria 125

The Holy Land

Israel's land has always been important. And that is an ironic truth. For this land even under King Solomon was not as large as our New England states. She has never marched her armies far from the homeland. Yet from earliest civilization this land has been involved in making world history. The key is found in its location. In one sense, God picked the center of the world for His chosen land. Israel stands on a bridge between three of the world's continents: Europe, Africa, and Asia. Powers from these continents have dominated world history. The vast Mediterranean Sea lies on Israel's west and a huge desert on its east, leaving this narrow strip of inhabitable, passable ground. So the ancient kingdoms from Egypt, Mesopotamia, and Europe all passed here in conquest of their worlds. They all considered Israel a prime and important piece of real estate. Controlling the Via Maris (Way of the Sea), as the route through Israel was called, was extremely important to trade. The land not only served as a frontier, buffer zone, or attack route, but also as a profitable business extracting tolls from the caravans that traveled between the major continents.

Even in our day of modern transportation and

warfare, and the emergence of three other significant continents, Israel is a key figure in world politics. After 2,000 years of wandering without a homeland, this people did not lose their identity or their culture, nor had they stopped praying, "next year Jerusalem." It is hard to read these words from Deuteronomy and not think of the past 2,000 years of Jewish history:

> *"And ye shall be left few in number, whereas ye were as the stars of heaven for multitude; because thou wouldest not obey the voice of the Lord thy God. And it shall come to pass, that as the Lord rejoiced over you to do you good, and to multiply you; so the Lord will rejoice over you to destroy you, and to bring you to nought; and ye shall be plucked from off the land whither thou goest to possess it. And the Lord shall scatter thee among all people, from the one end of the earth even unto the other; and there thou shalt serve other gods, which neither thou nor thy fathers have known, even wood and stone. And among these nations shalt thou find no ease, neither shall the sole of thy foot have rest: but the Lord shall give thee there a trembling heart, and failing of eyes, and sorrow of mind: And thy life shall hang in doubt before thee; and thou shalt fear day and night, and shalt have none assurance of thy life"*
> (Deut. 28:62-66)

> *"That then the Lord thy God will turn thy*

captivity, and have compassion upon thee, and will return and gather thee from all the nations, whither the Lord thy God hath scattered thee. If any of them be driven out unto the outmost parts of heaven, from thence will the Lord thy God gather thee, and from thence will he fetch thee: And the Lord thy God will bring thee into the land which thy fathers possessed, and thou shalt possess it; and he will do thee good, and multiply thee above thy fathers" (Deut. 30:3-5).

In 1948, by one vote, the United Nations passed a resolution making Israel a nation again!

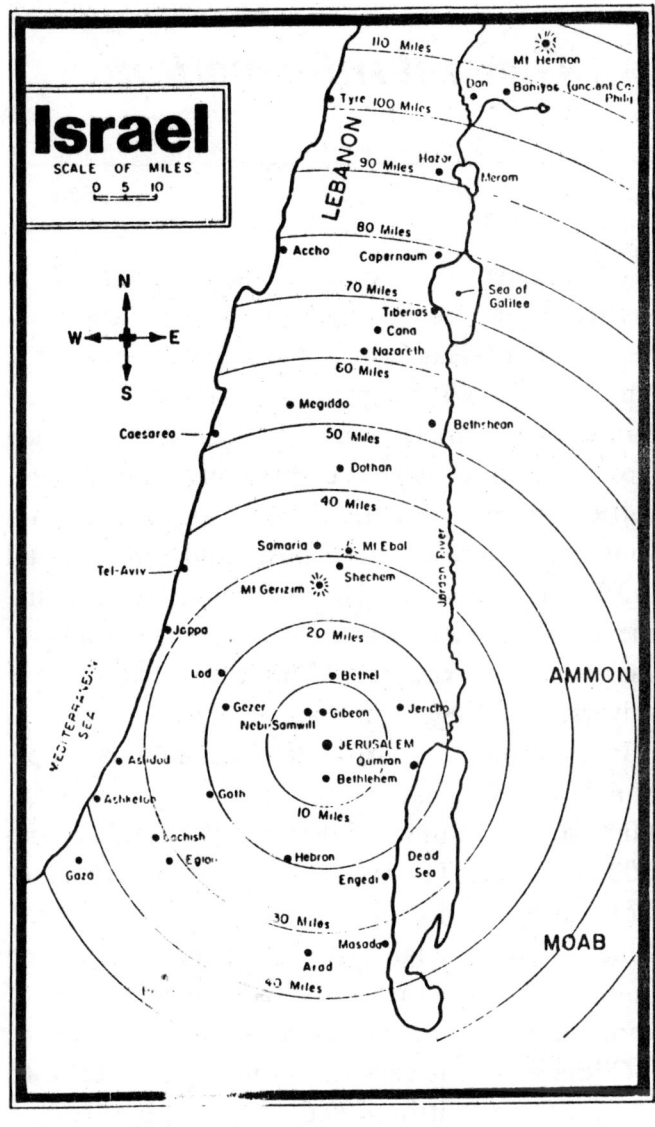

General Information

Government — The government of Israel is a republic. A president is elected by the Parliament (Knesset) for a 5-year term, but has no real power. The real power is held by the prime minister and a cabinet of ministers who are responsible to the Knesset which makes laws and keeps a close watch on all government activities. Members of the Knesset are elected on a proportional-representation basis and represent all the different groups in the Israeli population (including farmers, rabbis, lawyers, and Arabs). It is a unicameral house, with approximately 12 political parties. There is universal sufferage from the age of 18.

Population — Approximately 3 million people live in Israel. Of that figure, 2.9 million are Jews; 390,000 are Muslims; 85,000 are Christians; and 40,000 are Druze. Tel Aviv-Jaffa is the largest center of population with over 400,000. It is the cultural, commercial, and social center of modern Israel, even though Jerusalem is the capital. About 3.5 percent of the population live on collective farms.

Climate — It is very warm in the summer, with the Negev Desert hitting 120 degrees. Nights are cool in Jerusalem, even in the summer, because of its high altitude. Winter weather is cool with occasional frosts in Jerusalem, but there is virtually no snow.

Area — Before the June War of 1967, the area was ca. 8,000 square miles (the size of Massachusetts). Of this, 35 percent was arable; 19 percent was under cultivation; 60 percent was desert; and 3 percent was forests. Much has changed since that war. Today, Israel is 34,000 square miles (about the size of Maine or Indiana) since the addition of land in the Sinai and on the Golan Heights, as well as the West Bank territory. In an effort to re-forest their country, more than 50 million trees have been planted since 1948.

Natural Resources — *fisheries,* including commercial ponds, as well as the Sea of Galilee, the Jordan River, and the Mediterranean Sea; *agriculture,* including citrus fruits, wheat, barley, olives, cotton, grapes, and peanuts; *livestock,* including sheep, goats, cattle, horses, and donkeys; *minerals,* including copper, iron, potash, phosphates, rock salt, oil, and natural gas; and *tourism,* which is big business in Israel!

Education and Welfare — The official language is Hebrew, though Arabic is recognized as the official language of Arabs. English is taught in all schools, though the natives are hesitant to use it in front of Americans. Education is compulsory for all children ages 5-14. Youths who have not been to compulsory primary schooling must attend special classes. The Arabs and Jews have separate school systems. The country can boast of several excellent major universities. Israel has a national insurance program for illness, accident, and unemployment. The aged and disabled are also provided for through pensions.

Currency — The currency is built on the Israeli pound, which is broken into 100 agorots. The American dollar is worth _____ Israeli pounds.

History of the Name — The land area occupied by Israel has been primarily known by three names in the Scriptures: Canaan, Israel, and (KJV) Palestine. *Canaan* was used in the pre-conquest period. It refers to the land west of the Jordan River occupied by the 12 tribes after the conquest (Gen. 12:5; Num. 33:51). The term *Canaanite* refers to a trader or one who sells merchandise. The common occupation of this area probably initiated the labeling of the people and finally the land as Canaan. The product which made these people world-known was purple dye. The roots of the Canaanites are given in Genesis 10:15-19.

Israel was the name God gave to Jacob (Gen. 32:28, 49:2) and thus all his descendants. Jacob, even though he is the third patriarch, is the first in whom all descendants are part of the chosen race. Abraham and Isaac had children that would not be known as Israelites. So Jacob's new name is used as a synonym for Israel.

The name *Palestine* comes from the Philistine homeland, which runs from Gaza to Joppa on the Mediterranean coast. It was later used by secular writers to refer to the whole land in general. So through the ages the Holy Land has been referred to as Palestine. Though the King James text uses the term 4 times, later versions have more correctly translated the original as "Philistia."

Jewish Population Roots — The present day Jew in Israel probably comes from one of 4 backgrounds.

Ashkenazim (Hebrew for Germany) are Jews who come from Central and Eastern Europe. They spoke Yiddish, a compound of Hebrew and medieval German, and began coming in the sixteenth century. In those early days, they settled in Jerusalem, Hebron, Tiberias, or Tsefat.

Sefaradim (Hebrew for Spain) are Jews from Spain. They began migrating in the fifteenth century and spoke Ladino, a mixture of Spanish and Hebrew. Up until the nineteenth century, the greatest bulk of people in Israel were these.

Malaravim are Jews who came from the North African countries. They spoke Arabic with an African dialect.

A fourth group were the Jews who came from Jewish Oriental communities in Muslim countries like Yemen, Iran, and Iraq.

Moslems and Christians — The biggest minority in Israel are Moslems. They speak a Syrian dialect of Arabic. They have their own state schools, a daily newspaper, *Al Yom* (The Day), some are members in the Knesset, and they serve in the police force, but not in the army. Moslems are divided by their mode of life. There are villagers or tillers of the soil (most are in this category), townspeople who dwell in their own towns, though a few mix in the big cities, and

Bedouins, who live in tents and are breeders of sheep, goats, or camels. The Bedouins are the most unique. They are divided into tribes. At the head of each tribe is a sheik. He is the leader and also the representative in all tribal dealings with government institutions. Their own tribal court is empowered to act in the settlement of their internal disputes. Most dwell in the Negev and in Sinai, though a few tribes are scattered in the mountains of Galilee.

The bulk of the Christian population speaks Arabic, and its habits and mode of life are similar to those of its Arab neighbors. They are mostly Greek Orthodox or Catholic. Many of the Catholic orders have erected monasteries and convents on sites venerated in Christian tradition.

Types of Settlements — There are 4 forms of settlements in Israel. The first are cities, the most significant being Tel Aviv, Jerusalem, and Haifa. The second are *moshava* or villages. This was the first form of rural Jewish settlements. The third type are *moshav* or small holder settlements. There every settler lives separately with his family and tills a plot of land leased to him by the Jewish National Fund, where the village privately owns their land. In the small holder settlement a man is not allowed to hire workers. He must work the land with his family. The fourth type are *kibbutz* or *kevutsa*. They are purely collective. All members live and work together on national land leased to them by the Jewish National Fund. There is no private property.

General Information — 11

Land of the Gospels: Economical

Land of the Gospels: Travel Routes

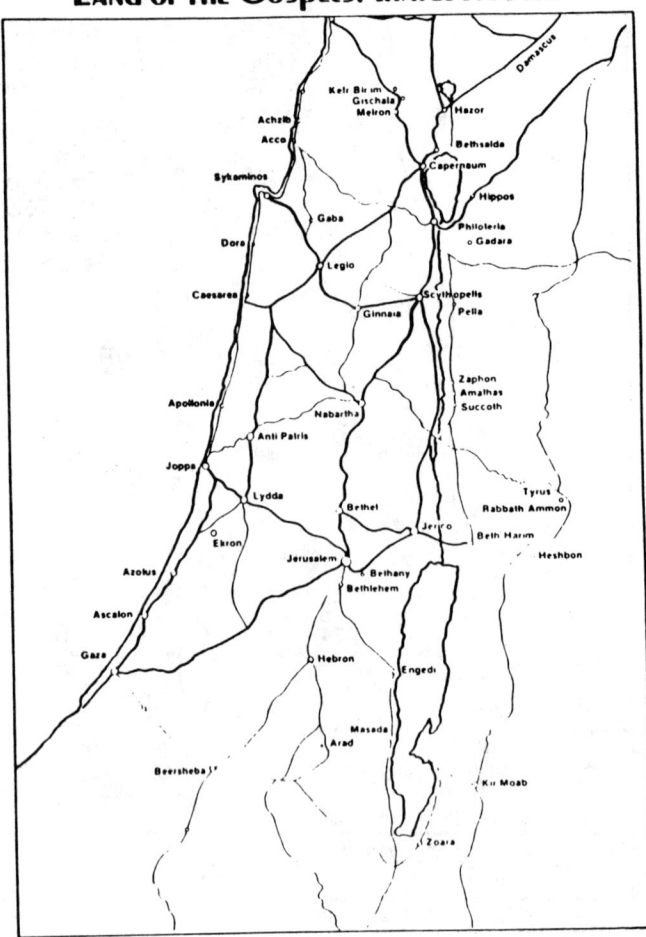

Israeli Agriculture

In Israel, climate and fertility are varied; therefore, cultivation, seedtime, and harvest differ in closely adjacent territories. On the coastal plains and in the Jordan Valley the soil is rich and the season early, but in the hill country the season runs the schedule at least 2 weeks to a month later. To use hill terracing is often necessary. In unwatered areas, crops are grown only in winter and spring (rainy seasons). These areas dry up in May and remain dry until it rains in October or so.

Some of the farming operations are identical to those used 2,000 years ago or more. This is especially true in grain and vegetable farming.

Grain Farming — Plains need little tilling, but rocks present a real problem in the hills (these are piled into fences around the field). Often, wooden plows are used. In some areas they are pulled by camels; in other areas they are pulled by donkeys; and in Samaria the Deuteronomic law was often broken by yoking an ox and an ass together for easier plowing.

Sowing — Seed was broadcast (Matt. 13:3) and then plowed again. Footpaths are respected and are left unbroken. Seed which falls here is eaten by birds.

Reaping — After sowing, the fields are deserted until after the winter rains, unless destroyed by rain or hail (Exod. 9:25). In April, barley ripens, and wheat follows 4-6 weeks later, depending upon altitude. About the end of May or the first of June when the dry season begins, reaping begins. Families move from village to field until harvest is over. Handfuls of grain are gathered together and are cut by a sickle. These handfuls are left behind and the "gleaners" (usually children) transport them to a threshing floor.

Threshing: Floors are constructed in the fields where they can have the full benefit of the winds (circular 25-40 feet in diameter, prepared by removing all stones, wetting the ground, tramping it, and sweeping it). A border of stones is laid. Sheaves of grain are cast here and tramping begins as animals and drags (studded with basalt stones underneath) are used to tread out the grain. The unthreshed grain is kept in the center and is cast into the path of the drag as the partly threshed grain is turned by a fork. Stalks become broken and blow away. The chaff and grain remaining are then winnowed (by tossing into the air to blow away the chaff). Then the grain is placed in wooden trays and the foreign articles are separated by hand, or a sifter can be used. Later it is placed in bags to be stored or made ready for the mill.

Vineyards: Grapes played an important part in people's diet. From July through September all Israelis considered them part of almost every meal in New Testament and Old Testament times. They were eaten fresh and made into wine. Often molasses is made from the grape juice. Most of the attention which this crop deserved could be given at times when the farmer was otherwise idle. Watchtowers were placed in vineyards to protect them from animals and robbers. Grapes were harvested and placed into winepresses where they were tread out by foot and the juice then stored in jars until it was served as fresh juice or fermented wine. Some grapes were served fresh and others dried for later meals.

Summary of Modern Israeli History

The British government gave up its mandate over Palestine in May of 1948. The United Nations voted to divide the land between the Arabs and the Jewish people, making Jerusalem an international city shared by all. The Arabs voiced their disapproval of the plan; the Jews were in favor of it. The date was set for May 14, 1948. The world knew that war would immediately break out and the Arab countries were heavily favored to crush the existence of any Jewish state. The first night of independence, Tel Aviv was bombed and the Arab armies marched into Israel. The war raged on for a year, finally ending with an armistice between Israel and Jordan, though the Arab countries have never recognized Israel as being any more than occupied Palestine.

In the summer of 1956 Egypt nationalized the Suez Canal, bringing Israeli/Arab tensions to a head. In the fall of that year Israel, along with Britain and France, attacked Egypt. Israel gained most of the land in the Sinai Peninsula, but it was later returned under pressure from the United States.

War again broke out in 1967, known as the Six-

Day War. Israel gained the Sinai, the West Bank, and the Golan Heights east of the Sea of Galilee. Most significant was the gaining of Jerusalem. Not since 1948 had the Jews been allowed to come to the Wailing Wall.

Finally, in 1973, Egypt and Syria staged a surprise attack on the Jewish holy day of Yom Kippur. The ensuing days proved disastrous for both sides, yet Israel recouped from this surprise attack and maintained its previous borders.

Outline of Israel's History

1. Before Abraham (e.g. Jericho) in existence.
2. Abraham ca. 2000 B.C.
3. Moses between 1400-1250 B.C.
4. David ca. 1000 B.C.
5. Assyrians overran ca. 722 B.C.
6. Babylonians ca. 586 B.C.
7. Persians ca. 540 B.C.
8. Greeks ca. 332 B.C.
9. Independent country ca. 167-62 B.C.
10. Roman rule — 63 B.C.-ca. A.D. 379.
11. Post-Roman or Byzantine Period; ca. A.D. 379-ca. 630; after the partition of the Roman Empire ca. A.D. 379, Palestine came under the rule of the Byzantine rulers.
12. Arab Period — ca. 630 — Jerusalem fell to Moslems in 638 — ca. 1099.
13. Crusader Period — ca. 1099-1250.
14. Mameluke Period (Egypt) — ca. 1250-1515.
15. Turkish Period — ca.1515-1917. Imp. of nineteenth century British and Jewish desires to set up a Jewish state in Palestine. Especially important was Theodor Herzl and the founding of the World Zionist Organization near the end of the nineteenth century and immigration of Jews from different

parts of the world to Palestine. In 1882 Palestine had a population of ca. 450,000, of which only about 24,000 were Jews. Mass migrations of Jews began from Russia, Romania, and Poland. By 1914 there were 85,000 Jews in Palestine.
16. British Mandate — 1917-1948. By 1925 there were 108,000 Jews in Palestine and when the Nazi power arose in Germany, thousands fled to Palestine (60,000 in 1935 alone). Trouble developed between Arabs and Jews. In 1939 tens of thousands reached Palestine from Europe.
17. United Nations — On May 14, 1948, the British mandate over Palestine ended and the State of Israel officially began. It passed a law to permit Jews to return. In 1949 alone 239,076 arrived; in 1950, 109,405; and in 1951, 174,019.

 The U.N. General Assembly had voted on November 29, 1947 to divide Palestine into Jewish and Arab states to become effective upon the withdrawal of the British in 1949.

 War broke out immediately between Jews and Arabs and lasted until 1949. The country remained divided, as did the city of Jerusalem, until the Six-Day War in June 1967. Since then, the Jews have occupied all of Jerusalem and all land west of the Jordan River as far north as Lebanon and the Sinai Peninsula down to the Suez Canal.

 War again broke out in the fall of 1973, known as the "Yom Kippur War." Israeli troops crossed the Suez Canal and were within striking distance of Cairo (less than 100 miles) when cease-fire came. Israel occupied more Syrian territory in the Golan Heights area (northeast of the Sea of Galilee) and were within striking distance of Damascus when cease-fire came.

Geographical Area

22 — *Israel and the Holy Land*

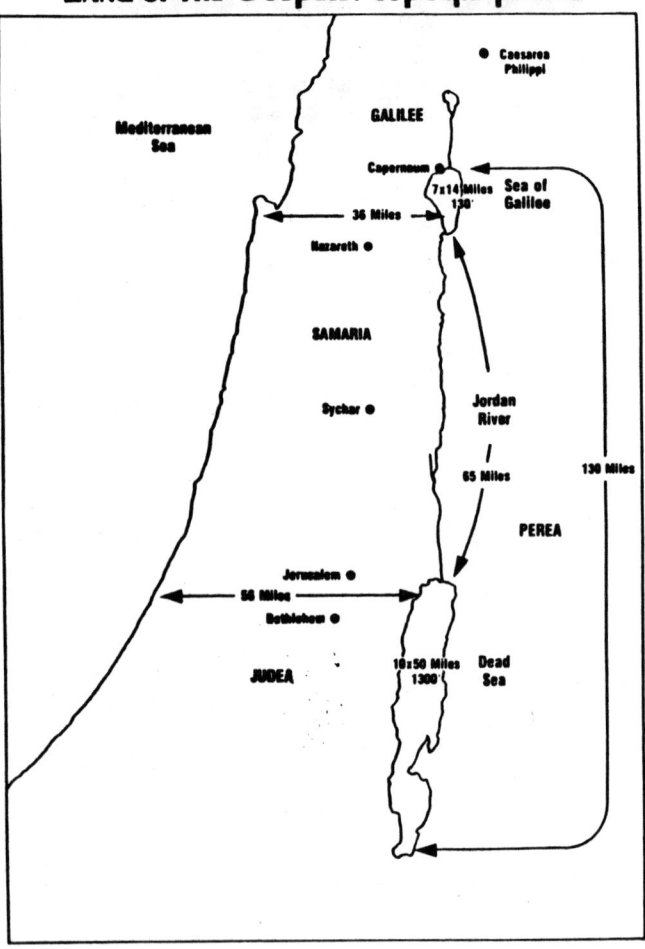

Topography of Israel

West to East

Viewing the topography of Israel from west to east, from the Mediterranean to the Jordan, five general types are normally listed.

Coastal Plain — This land is in the extreme west; it narrows as you travel north until it almost ends at Haifa, where the Carmel mountain runs to the sea. It begins again north of Haifa and runs up into Lebanon. Israel did little with this land in the beginning since it had little use for farmers and herdsmen. It was hard to defend and frequently was used by foreign travelers. Not until David conquered the Philistines did Israel really control it.

Shephelah — Bordering on the coastal plain as we move east is the shephelah. The shephelah is a belt of gently rolling hills between 500 and 1,000 feet high. It acted as a buffer between the plains and the higher mountains. Israel's primary dwelling place during most of her history was in the higher mountains, or heartland as it is called. This belt of lower hills is widest in the south and disappears as you travel north of Jerusalem. It served as a buffer zone to Israel from attacking enemies. This gave the Southern Kingdom a much more defensible position than the Northern Kingdom.

Mountain Spine or Heartland — Israel has a line of mountains running north-south. This was the heart of Israeli occupation. Even her enemies thought of her as hill people. In 1 Kings 20:23, Syria reasoned it was suffering defeat when it fought Israel in the hills because their God had power in the hills. So it determined to make Israel fight in the plains where her God would be powerless. The mountains are broadest in the south at Hebron and run north until Mt. Gilboa where the Valley of Armageddon begins. There the mountains turn northwest and run to the Mediterranean Sea at Haifa. The mountains continue again north of the valley and up into Lebanon.

Jordan Rift — Whereas the west side of the mountain spine drops off gently, the east side drops off precipitously into the Jordan Valley. The Jordan Valley is part of a great geological rift that runs from Lebanon 3,000 miles south into Southern Africa. At the Sea of Galilee the surface is already 600 feet below sea level, and by the time we get to the Dead Sea the surface is 1,300 feet below sea level. This is the lowest spot on the earth's surface. Because of its altitude it has a tropical climate.

Trans-Jordan — There is a belt of mountains 30-50 miles in width on the east side of the Jordan River. This spine of mountains generally increases in height as it goes south. The mountains east of Galilee are approximately 2,000 feet high, while those in Edom rise to 5,000 feet in height, yet rainfall decreases as you travel south. The land across from Galilee is extremely good agricultural land. It is still good across from Samaria but more suited to pasture land as it is more hilly. The Moab area would be used chiefly for herding sheep and goats.

26 — *Israel and the Holy Land*

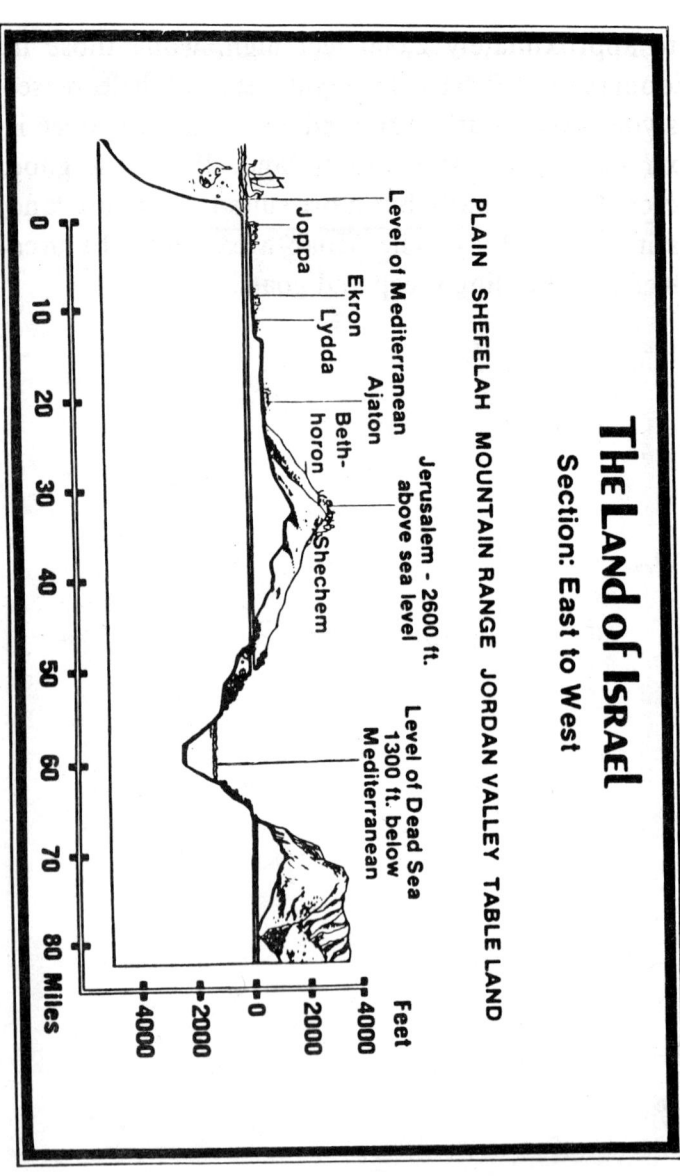

Topography of Israel — 27

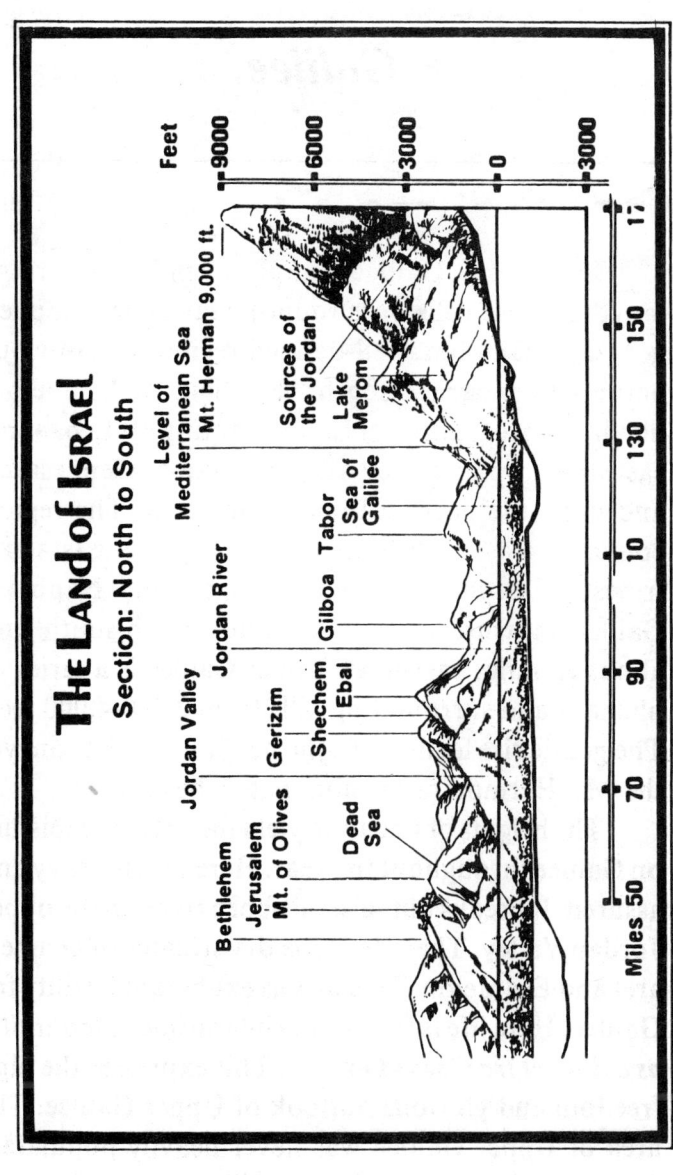

Galilee

The name Galilee simply means "the ring" (anything that rolls or is round). Galilee was applied geographically to a well-defined region with obvious natural boundaries: south, the Plain of Esdraelon; north, the great gorge of Litany (cutting off Lebanon); east, the Jordan Valley and the Lake of Gennesaret; and west, the narrow Phoenician coast. The region coincides closely with the territories of four Israelite tribes — Issachar, Zebulum, Asher, and Naphtali. Galilee measured about 50 miles north-south and about 25 miles east-west. Upper Galilee is a series of plateaus and surrounding hills from 2,000-4,000 feet. The gentle rise leads up to the heights of Lebanon, yet the Mt. Hermon range dominates the area.

The heights of Lebanon yield their stored moisture on Galilee throughout the year. Here rain is heavy and assured. It breaks out into full-born rivers in the upper Jordan Valley. These feed the dry streams of Gennesaret and Esdraelon. This means exuberant fertility for Galilee. Here life is free and exhilarating. *"Naphtali is as a doe set free"* says Genesis. This expresses the high freedom and glorious outlook of Upper Galilee. The area of Upper Galilee was never heavily populated. But in dry Lower Galilee the villages were frequent and there were many fortified towns. The population was numerous in Jesus' day.

Galilee was unique for the breaks in her massive limestone ranges by volcanic extrusions and extinct craters. Basalt rock is found in every lake and on the plateaus. Hot sulphur springs gush up at Tiberias and often in history the whole province has been shaken by earthquakes. Palestine was divided into a number of regions, each very small, but sharply different from one another. Each possessed a very definite local consciousness. The people of Judea, of Samaria, and of Galilee lived apart and their interests were very different. Though they traveled through other regions, they were most loyal to their own communities, and they resented the claims of others.

The nature of the people of Galilee was also volcanic. We remember two Galileans who wished to call down fire from heaven on those who were discourteous to them (Luke 9:54). Yet, Galileans were a chivalrous and gallant race (Jud. 5:18). The same desperate zeal was a part of their sons who attempted to break the Roman power. As Josephus says,

"The country was never destitute of men with courage."

For these causes, perhaps, our Lord chose His friends from these people.

Galilee, "this garden of our Lord," was crossed by many of the world's famous highways. The great west road from Damascus to the Mediterranean Sea was the famous Via Maris (Way of the Sea). The Romans paved it and collected tolls at Capernaum where Matthew "sat at the receipt of customs" (Mark 2:14). It was a great trade route with Far Eastern products passing daily over its surface. The great road of the east from Acre to Lower Galilee at Behshan and into Gilead often carried Roman troops and merchants. Up and down these roads the immortal figures of the parables passed: merchants seeking goodly pearls; kings departing to receive kingdoms; the householder arriving suddenly on the wicked servants; and even the "prodigal son." The roads caused the world of Jesus to touch Rome and even Babylon.

Galilee came into its own in New Testament times. It was then under stern Roman control but this had freed these hills from fear of enemy attack. The region had a consciousness of its own and a tendency toward independent thought, encouraged by easy contacts with the outside world. Thus, the Jews in the south despised the Jews of Galilee and felt certain that no prophet could arise from such a free-thinking group (John 1:46; 7:41, 52). Yet it was here that Jesus chose to teach, rather than in the area of the true center of Judaism, Jerusalem. Here he chose his closest disciples.

We are told that Jesus walked all over Galilee from village to village, skirted fertile basins which were rich with grain, and climbed among olive trees which clothed the slopes. He trudged the dusty summer footpaths and met farmers with their laden donkeys taking produce to the village markets. He traveled in the grey cool hours and in very early dawn. Sometimes He used the great trade routes, yet most often turned onto narrow tracks leading to the Galilean villages He loved, even His hometown of Nazareth. Of all the villages visited by Jesus, only three are mentioned in the New Testament: Nazareth, Cana, and Nain.

Biblical References

Kedesh, one of the cities of refuge was here — *"And they appointed Kedesh in Galilee in mount Naphtali . . ."* (Josh. 20:7).

Solomon gave Hiram 20 cities in this land — *"Now Hiram the king of Tyre had furnished Solomon with cedar trees and fir trees, and with gold, according to all his desire, that then king Solomon gave Hiram twenty cities in the land of Galilee"* (1 Kings 9:11).

Jesus did most of His earthly ministry in Galilee — *"But when he heard that Archelaus did reign in Judea in the room of his father Herod, he was afraid to go thither: notwithstanding, being warned of God in a dream, he turned aside into the parts of Galilee"* (Matt. 2:22).

Peter and Andrews were called from Galilee — *"And*

Jesus, walking by the sea of Galilee, saw two brethren, Simon called Peter, and Andrew his brother, casting a net into the sea: for they were fishers. And he saith unto them, Follow me, and I will make you fishers of men. And they straightway left their nets, and followed him" (Matt. 4:18-20).

Jesus preached and healed many here — *"And Jesus went about all Galilee, teaching in their synagogues, and preching the gospel of the kingdom, and healing all manner of sickness and all manner of disease among the people. And his fame went throughout all Syria: and they brought unto him all sick people that were taken with divers diseases and torments, and those which were possessed with devils, and those which were lunatick, and those that had the palsy; and he healed them. And there followed him great multitudes of people from Galilee, and from Decapolis and from Jerusalem, and from Judea, and from beyond Jordan"* (Matt. 4:23-25).

Christ said He would go here after His resurrection — *"Then saith Jesus unto them, All ye shall be offended because of me this night: for it is written, I will smite the shepherd, and the sheep of the flock shall be scattered abroad. But after I am risen again, I will go before you into Galilee"* (Matt. 26:31-32).

Joseph went from here to Bethlehem to be taxed — *"And Joseph also went up from Galilee, out of the city of Nazareth, into Judea, unto the city of David, which is called Bethlehem; (because he was of the house and lineage of David)"* (Luke 2:4).

Jesus came in the power of the Spirit to Galilee — *"And Jesus returned in the power of the Spirit into Galilee: and there went out a fame of him through all the region round about"* (Luke 4:14).

Jesus preached in the synagogues of Galilee — *"And he preached in the synagogues of Galilee"* (Luke 4:44).

Jesus performed His first miracle of His earthly ministry in Galilee — *"And the third day there was a marriage in Cana of Galilee; and the mother of Jesus was there . . . This beginning of miracles did Jesus of Cana of Galilee, and manifested forth his glory; and his disciples believed on him"* (John 2:1, 11).

Jesus went to Galilee when the Jews sought to kill Him — *"After these things Jesus walked in Galilee: for he would not walk in Jewry, because the Jews sought to kill him"* (John 7:1).

Jesus revealed Himself as Christ in Galilee — *"Then cried Jesus in the temple as he taught, saying, Ye both know me, and ye know whence I am: and I am not come of myself, but he that sent me is true, whom ye know not. But I know him: for I am from him, and he hath sent me"* (John 7:28-29).

Plain of Esdraelon

This is also called the Valley of Jezreel. The Plain of Esdraelon is a great plain in central Palestine lying between Mt. Gilboa and Mt. Tabor on the east and Mt. Carmel on the west. It extends from Mt. Carmel to the Jordan Valley. Average elevation is 200 feet above sea leve. The bed of the Kishon River lies in the plain and runs into the Mediterranean Sea at Mt. Carmel. In winter during the rains, the area around the Kishon is soft mud. (This probably happened during the battle of Sisera. As the modern calvary floundered in the morass they were easy prey for the foot soldiers of Israel.)

The plain is extremely fertile, being excellent land for crops, while trees flourish in the foothills nearby (especially olive trees). The plain belonged to the tribe of Issachar (Josh. 19:17). The valley has played a very important part in history due to the avenues of communication that crossed its breadth. Here opposing armies met often in deadly strife.

There were probably many battles waged in the plain in ancient times, but no records were left behind. The first recorded battle was that of Sisera's host being overthrown (Jud. 5:20). They were surprised and routed by Gideon's 300 chosen men in the stretches of the northern plain (Jud. 7). Near here Saul was defeated by the Philistines and he and his sons (Jonathan included) perished on Mt. Gilboa (1 Sam. 31). In the bed of the Kishon River at the foot of Mt. Carmel Elijah slaughtered the prophets of Baal (1 Kings 18:40). Ahab's household was destroyed by the furiously driving Jehu at Jezreel. Ahaziah was killed at Megiddo (2 Kings 9). Near Megiddo, Pharoah-nechoh slew Josiah in 610 B.C. (2 Kings 23:30; 2 Chron. 35:20).

The inspired writer of Revelation (Rev. 16:14, 16) placed the scene of the final war in the *"great day of God"* in the area often colored crimson, in the place called "Har-Magedon" or the "Mount of Megiddo."

Samaria

The area of Samaria is also called Mt. Ephraim. The patriarchs came first to Shechem; the earliest seats of Israel's worship, the earliest rallies of her patriotism were on Mt. Ephraim. Yet, the bulk of literature speaks of her with scorn, mentioning her traffic of foreigners, her luxury, and her tolerance of idols.

The earliest name given to the central range was Mt. Ephraim. Viewed from Gilead east of Jordan, it was an isolated group of hills, but viewed from the Mediterranean Sea it looked like a single mountain. Her western flank had summits to 3,000 feet with an average watershed height of 2,000 feet. The general aspect is rocky and sterile with frequent breaks of olive woods, fields, and villages. Only a little history has been enacted on her slopes here. On her eastern flank the descent is about 2,800 feet in less than 9 miles (3 times the gradient of the western slope). Here the hills fall close to the Jordan River.

Samaria's openness is her prominent feature and it tells her story. Few invaders were successfully resisted. Among such invaders were: the Canaanites, the Midianites (in Gideon's day), the Syrians almost annually (in Elisha's day), and the Assyrians who overwhelmed the land and carried off its population. Under the Romans came Vespasian and Titus with many others until our modern day.

Antipathy between the Jews and the Samaritans dates from the breakup of the Hebrew kingdoms. When Solomon died, civil war broke out, resulting in the division of the nation: 10 tribes formed the Northern Kingdom of Israel, with its capital at Samaria; Judah and Benjamin formed the Southern Kingdom, with its capital at Jerusalem. In the year 721 B.C., Sargon captured Samaria. Samaria was then the capital of the 10 tribes of the Northern Kingdom of Israel. Sargon located these people partly in Gozan and partly in cities recently captured from the Medes. This was a complete evacuation of the country. It was wiped clean of its inhabitants, which was not unusual among the customs of the Oriental conquerors. The country was left in a desolate condition and the warfared desolation allowed wild beasts to get the upper hand. In 677 B.C. Esar-haddon, during one of his invasions of Judah, perceived the idea of moving a garrison of foreigners back into the area which was once called Samaria, or the Northern Kingdom. He thus gathered men from Babylon, from Cuthahava, and from Hamath. All of these people then settled in the land that was once occupied by the 10 tribes.

These strangers, as is mentioned in Luke 17:18 from the Far East were, of course, idolators. They worshipped various deities and not knowing the God of the land they provoked Him, they thought, by their heathenish rites; and they believed that the God of the land sent lions to devour them. Many of them were slain, as is mentioned in 2 Kings 17:25. In their distress, they applied to the king of Assyria, and he sent to them one of the captive priests who originally came from the land to instruct them in "how they should fear the Lord." Under this priest's teachings they acknowledged Jehovah as God and He was added to the list of their ancient idols. Yet, in the course of time, they detached themselves more and more from the heathen customs and they adopted a sort of worship of Jehovah. These people, in time, intermarried and intermingled with the society of the children of Israel that had been left behind in the deportation. Out of the amalgamation of these elements sprang up the Samaritan people.

A great number of the Jews were returned from the captivity. They located themselves in the area of Jerusalem. The Samaritans at that time were refused permission to participate in the rebuilding of the Temple, and they became open enemies of the Jews. The Samaritans, in turn, erected a rival temple upon Mt. Gerizim. The Samaritan religion, even at that time, was based upon the Pentateuch, and its cult was centered in the temple of Mt. Gerizim. Indeed, where the Hebrew text of Deuteronomy 27:4 records the divine command that after crossing the Jordan River into the promised land the Israelites were to build a stone altar on Mt. Ebal for burnt offerings, the Samaritan Pentateuch substituted Mt. Gerizim for

Mt. Ebal. The reason is to be found in Deuteronomy 11:29 and Deuteronomy 27:12, where Ebal is the Mount of Cursing and Gerizim is the Mount of Blessing. They continued to worship on Mt. Gerizim until it was destroyed by John Hyrcanus in 130 B.C. Later they built another temple in Shechem under the modern name of Nablus. There today they have a settlement consisting of more than 200 persons. Gradually these Samaritan people detached themselves from the ancient idolatries. The Samaritans adopted the Mosaic religion, but received of the Scriptures only the Pentateuch, rejecting every other book of the Jewish camp. They celebrated the Passover on Mt. Gerizim (and still do today). Even after their temple fell into the hands of John Hyrcanus, they directed their worship toward Mt. Gerizim.

They held a doctrine of the coming Messiah. They called Him Ajshad or "The Converter." They founded this doctrine upon the words of Moses in Deuteronomy 18:15. They differed with regard to the characteristics of the Messiah. They ridiculed the Jewish idea of His being a King and a great conqueror. His mission, they said, was not to shed blood, but to heal the nations; not to make war, but to bring peace. He was to be according to the Mosaic promise, a great teacher, a restorer of the law, and one who would bring all the nations to unite under one in the service of one God. They believed His mission was to turn the ungodly and the unbelieving unto the Lord. They also believed that He would restore the glory of the holy law on Mt. Gerizim. The Samaritans thus had formed a halfway house between Judaism and the Gentile world proper. They were a heterogeneous people of mixed Israelitish and heathen blood. But their religion was genuinely Israelitish. They worshipped Yahweh, they kept the Sabbath, and they practiced circumcision. Their holy place, of course, was Mt. Gerizim. Though they were hated and despised by their Jewish neighbors, they were not put upon the level with the heathen. Their observance of the law was regarded as very defective, but they were not as complete aliens of the law.

    The feud ripened later, especially during the New Testament days into hostilities of the most bitter description. The Jews were perpetually reminding the Samaritans that they were "Cuthites" or "mere strangers from Assyria." They loved to call them "proselytes of lions" referring to 2 Kings 17:25. They liked to accuse them of worshipping the idol gods buried many ages ago under the oak of Shechem, found in Genesis 35:4. The Jews accused them publicly and cursed them in their synagogues. The Jews said that any who entered into a Samaritan house was laying up judgments upon his own children. And to eat a morsel of food from a Samaritan house was to eat of swine's flesh. They refused to receive the Samaritan as a proselyte and they declared that he would have no part in the resurrection of the dead. In traveling from north to south, Jews always preferred to take the long circuit through Perea rather than pass through the hated Samaritan country.

The Samaritans, on the other hand, refused hospitality to the pilgrim companies going to the feast at Jerusalem. You might compare this to Luke 9:53. Josephus said that sometimes the Samaritans would even waylay and murder the Jews. On one occasion, it is said that some Samaritans entered into the Temple at Jerusalem and defiled it by scattering human bones all over the pavement. Some of the inhospitality shown to the Jewish people was shown to Jesus and His disciples (Luke 9:51-56). The Jews were in the habit of communicating to their numerous brethren in Babylon on the exact day and hour of the rising of the Passover moon, or Paschal moon. They did this by means of a system of beacon fires, which telegraphed the news from the Mt. of Olives. The Samaritans would annoy the watchers in Babylon on the mountain tops by kindling a rival flame on the wrong day. This would perplex them and introduce confusion. Thus the Samaritans were a hated people by the Jews. They were a race apart.

Jesus Christ tells the story of the good Samaritan when a lawyer questioned Him, asking "Who is my brother?" Phillip left Jerusalem in a new mood to preach the gospel in Samaria as well as Judea. This new move involved no definite breach with the Jewish law, but revealed a concern for the Samaritans that no ordinary Jew would feel. It marked an advance on the spirit of Judaism in general, and an approach to Jesus on broader sympathy toward all mankind.

The Samaritan race today is ruled by a high priest whose predecessor centuries ago was a rival to the high priest of the Temple in Jerusalem. They worship in the synagogue according to their ancient and peculiar law, accepting only the first 5 books of Moses, or the Pentateuch. Their most treasured possession is an ancient copy of the Pentateuch written on lamb's skin, claimed to have been written by Aaron, the brother of Moses. (This is extremely doubtful.) Each year the Samaritans, even today, sacrifice lambs on top of their holy mountain, Gerizim. The extraordinary feast is carried out exactly as the Passover was carried out in the Old Testament days. The entire community leaves its homes and they camp out on top of the mountain. On the eve of the Passover, as the full moon rises, the high priest intones the prayers and the slayers draw their knives, slitting the throats of the innocent lambs; a disgusting but historically fascinating ceremony, the last relic of the ritual of ancient Israel. The tent doors are smeared with blood. Lambs are roasted and then eaten. The Samaritans gulp down the meat in large mouthfuls to simulate the haste with which the Israelites were sent out from Egypt.

The Samaritans today are an interesting people. Still the Jews, as in Jesus' day, reject friendship with this crossbred race. An understanding of such an outlook in the New Testament is extremely important to the interpretation of the Scriptures whenever the name Samaritan is mentioned. Such holds true for the

Old Testament, even as for the New Testament.

Biblical References

Here was the pleasure-loving court of Ahab and his queen Jezebel, and here Ahab built a temple to Baal — *"And in the thirty and eighth year of Asa king of Judah began Ahab the son of Omri to reign over Israel: and Ahab the son of Omri reigned over Israel in Samaria twenty and two years. And Ahab the son of Omri did evil in the sight of the Lord above all that were before him. And it came to pass . . . that he took to wife Jezebel . . . and went and served Baal, and worshipped him. And he reared up an alter for Baal in the house of Baal, which he had built in Samaria"* (1 Kings 16:29-33).

Elijah appeared in the streets of Samaria before Ahab and proclaimed the vengeance of Jehovah against the king — *"And Elijah the Tishbite, who was of the inhabitants of Gilead, said unto Ahab, As the Lord God of Israel liveth, before whom I stand, there shall not be dew nor rain these year, but according to my word"* (1 Kings 17:1).

Ahab's family was killed in Samaria by Jehu, who also destroyed the temple of Baal — *"And when he [Jehu] came to Samaria, he slew all that remained unto Ahab in Samaria, till he had destroyed him, according to the saying of the Lord, which he spake to Elijah. And they brought forth the images out of the house of Baal, and burned them. And they brake down the image of Baal and brake down the house of Baal . . . Thus Jehu destroyed Baal out of Israel"* (2 Kings 10:17, 26-28).

Here Jesus healed the 10 lepers — *"And it came to pass, as he went to Jerusalem, that he passed through the midst of Samaria and Galilee. And as he entered into a certain village, there met him ten men that were lepers . . . And it came to pass, that, as they went, they were cleansed . . . And one of them . . . giving him thanks . . . was a Samaritan"* (Luke 17:11-19).

Here Jesus witnessed to the women at Jacob's Well, and the whole city was saved as a result — *"And he must needs go through Samaria. There cometh a woman of Samaria to draw water . . ."* (John 4:4, 7).

The disciples were instructed to be witnesses in Samaria — *"But ye shall receive power after that the Holy Ghost is come upon you: and ye shall be witnesses unto me both in Jerusalem, and in all Judaea, and in Samaria, and unto the uttermost part of the earth"* (Acts 1:8).

Peter, John, and Philip preached and ministered in the villages of Samaria — *"Now when the apostles which were at Jerusalem heard that Samaria had received the word of God, they sent unto them Peter and John: And they, when they had testified and preached the word of the Lord, returned to Jerusalem, and preached the gospel in many villages of the Samaritans"* (Acts 8:14, 25).

Ha-Negeb

The Negeb lays to the south of Judah, thus designated as "the South" (Gen. 13:1, 14). It is bounded on the east by the Dead Sea and the Arabah, and on the west by the Mediterranean Sea and the Sinai deserts. It has little rainfall and few springs, yet grazing is plentiful in the early spring months before the summer drought begins. It is a land of nomads with only a few other inhabitants, yet abundant ruins testify to heavy populations during some periods. The best trade routes pass along the coast on the west and then the Arabah on the east. The deserts of the south secured the boundaries of Judah from attack during all her history, nor could Israel even enter the land of the Amalekites from this direction (Num. 13:29; 14:43-45).

The Negeb was the scene of much of Abram's wanderings (Gen. 12:9; 13:1-3; 20:1). Here Hagar met the angel (Gen. 16:7, 14). Isaac and Jacob later both dwelt there (Gen. 24:62; 37:1; 46:5). Moses sent spies through this district to Canaan beyond (Num. 13:17, 22). Simeon was given the northern Negeb as his inheritance (Josh. 19:1-9). Many of David's exploits were against the Negeb of Judah, Jerahmeelites, and Kenites, and in 1 Samuel 30:14 there is mention of the

Negeb of Caleb and the Cherethites. Judges 1:16 mentions the Negeb of Arad. Jeremiah 17:26; 32:44; and 33:13 mention the area. (Also see Lam. 4:21; Ezek. 35:3-15; Josh. 15:21-32; 19:1-9; 1 Chron. 4:28-33; 1 Sam. 15:9; 27:9; 30:16; 2 Chron. 14:14).

Wilderness of Judea

The country bordering on the shores of the Dead Sea for some miles inland was known as the wilderness of Judea (Matt. 3:1), or "wilderness" in Mark 1:4 and Luke 3:2. In this area, John the Baptist preached and baptized.

Jordan River

About 6-7 miles from Jericho lies the Jordan River. It was probably in this vicinity (the exact site is not known) where Jesus was baptized by John the Baptist (Matt. 3:1).

The Headwaters — Jordan means "flowing down." It begins at the junction of 4 streams in the upper plain of Lake Huleh. The 4 tributaries of the Jordan River are as follows:

1. *Bareighit* — obtaining its waters from the hills of modern Lebanon and the furthest west,
2. *Hasbany* — the longest (40 miles), issuing from a great fountain at the western foot of Mt. Herman and descending 1,500 feet to the plain below,
3. *Leddan* — the largest, from several fountains at the foot of the ancient city of Dan, 505 feet above sea level, and
4. *Banias* — from the celebrated fount near Caesarea Philippi. The name Banias comes from a corruption of the word "paneas," for there is a grotto in this area dedicated to the pagan god Pan. Here Herod erected a palace to Augustus Caesar. The altitude is 1,100 feet above sea level, and the stream falls 600 feet in 5 miles.

Lake Huleh — The Huleh basin is the converging point of the 4 streams. The basin is 20 miles long and 5 miles wide with the mountains on either side rising 3,000 feet. After a 4-5 mile flow through the Huleh basin, the Jordan enters a morass of marshy land which once nearly filled the valley (today the malaria area is well drained and fish ponds and farm lands are the result of modern Israel's labors). In the previous morass, bushes and papyrus reeds hindered any navigation. Lake Huleh is 7 feet above sea level. At the southern end the valley narrows to only a few hundred yards and the river is only about 60 feet broad.

The Jordan River appears 195 times in the Bible! The Jordan is the only large, flowing body of water in Palestine. It has played an important part in the history of Israel. The Jordan is best described by Professor Glueck when he said:

"Squirming frantically, burrowing madly, seeking wildly to escape its fate, the Jordan courses, from its crystal clear beginning, to its literally dark and bitter end, in a helpless race to a hopeless goal."

The Jordan ranges from 90-100 feet wide, and from 3-10 feet deep.

Biblical References

The most important event relating to the Jordan River in the entire history of Israel is the crossing of the Jordan by Israel after the death of Moses — *"Speak unto the children of Israel, and say unto them, When ye be come over Jordan into the land of Canaan"* (Num. 35:10).

"Until the Lord have given rest unto your brethren, as well as unto you, and until they also possess the land which the Lord your God hath given them beyond Jordan: and then shall ye return every man unto his possession, which I have given you" (Deut. 3:20).

"For ye shall pass over Jordan to go in to possess the land which the Lord your God giveth you, and ye shall possess it, and dwell therein" (Deut. 11:31).

"Moses my servant is dead; now therefore arise, go over this Jordan, thou, and all this people, unto the land of the Hittites, and unto the great sea toward the going down of the sun, shall be your coast" (Josh. 1:2, 4).

Jordan is first mentioned in the Bible in Genesis 13, where Lot chose the plain of Jordan for his possession and he and Abraham parted ways — *"And Lot lifted up his eyes, and beheld all the plain of Jordan, that was well watered every where, before the Lord destroyed Sodom and Gomorrah, even as the garden of the Lord, like the land of Egypt, as thou comest unto Zoar. Then Lot chose him all the plain of Jordan; and Lot journeyed east: and they separated themselves the one from the other"* (Gen. 13:10-11).

The great text in Numbers 32 was given by Moses to the Reubenites and Gadites if they refused to cross Jordan and help their brethren subdue the land — *"And Moses said unto them, If ye will do this thing, if ye will go armed before the Lord to war, And will go all of you armed over Jordan before the Lord, until he hath driven out his enemies from before him, And the land be subdued before the Lord: then afterward ye shall return, and be guiltless before the Lord, and before Israel; and this land shall be your possession before the Lord. But if ye will not do so, behold, ye have sinned against the Lord: and be sure your sin will find you out. Build you cities for your little ones, and folds for your sheep; and do that which hath proceeded out of your mouth"* (Num. 32:20-24).

The Jordan River stood up in a heap, and stood still until Israel crossed over, following the priests bearing the Ark — *"And it came to pass, when the people removed from their tents, to pass over Jordan, and the priests bearing the ark of the covenant before the people; And as they that bare the ark were come unto Jordan, and the feet of the priests that bare the ark were dipped in the brim of the water, (for Jordan overfloweth all his banks all the time of harvest,) That the waters which came down from above stood and rose up upon an heap very far from the city Adam, that is beside Zaretan: and those that came down toward the sea of the plain, even the salt sea, failed, and were cut off: and the people passed over right against Jericho. And the priests that bare the ark of the covenant of the Lord stood firm on dry ground in the midst of Jordan, and all the Israelites passed over on dry ground, until all the people were passed clean over Jordan"* (Josh. 3:14-17).

Absalom passed over Jordan in pursuit of his father, David — *"Then David came to Mahanaim. And Absalom passed over Jordan, he and all the men of Israel with him"* (2 Sam. 17:24).

David passed over Jordan on his return to Jerusalem — *"So the king returned and came to Jordan. And Judah came to Gilgal, to go to meet the king, to conduct the king over Jordan. And Shimei the son of Gera, a Benjamite, which was of Bahurim, hasted and came down with the men of Judah to meet king David. And there were a thousand men of Benjamin with him, and Ziba the servant of the house of Saul, and his fifteen sons and his twenty servants with him; and they went over Jordan before the king. And there went over a ferry boat to carry over the king's household, and to do what he thought good. And Shimei the son of Gera fell down before the king, as he was come over Jordan"* (2 Sam. 19:15-18).

Elijah was fed by the ravens by the brook Cherith, which is before Jordan — *"And the word of the Lord came unto him, saying, Get thee hence, and turn thee eastward, and hide thyself by the brook Cherith, that* is before Jordan. And it shall be, that thou shalt drink of the brook; and I have commanded the ravens to feed thee there. So he went and did according unto the word of the Lord: for he went and dwelt by the brook Cherith, that is before Jordan" (1 Kings 17:2-5).

Jesus was baptized in Jordan — "Then cometh Jesus from Galilee to Jordan unto John, to be baptized of him. But John forbad him, saying, I have need to be baptized of thee, and comest thou to me? And Jesus answering said unto him, Suffer it to be so now: for thus it becometh us to fulfill all righteousness. Then he suffered him. And Jesus, when he was baptized, went up straightway out of the water: and, lo, the heavens were opened unto him, and he saw the Spirit of God descending like a dove, and lighting upon him: And lo a voice from heaven, saying, This is my beloved Son, in whom I am well pleased" (Matt. 3:13-17).

Sea of Galilee

In the New Testament the Sea of Galilee is also known as the Sea of Tiberias, the Lake of Gennesaret, the Sea, and the Lake. In the Old Testament it is also known as the Sea of Chinnereth and Sea of Chinneroth.

The Sea of Galilee is 680 feet below sea level due east of the Bay of Acre, 13 miles long, 5½-8 miles wide, 32½ miles in circumference, and 150 feet deep at the deepest point. It is called the Lake of Tiberias, Tov Reiya in Hebrew meaning "beautiful view" or the Sea of Kinneret (Chinnereth), Kinnor in Hebrew for "harp." Many said the waves sound like the voice of a harp and the sea is shaped like a harp. The water is clear and sweet. It looks like a sapphire in a setting of emerald. It is shut in by hills on every side with the broadest plain being the Gennesaret to the northwest as the hills withdraw a little from the shore.

This area has warm winters (never frosts) and long hot summers (with east winds, it gets as hot as 114 degrees in the shade). It has rich production of all kinds of Palestinian crops and plentiful water. In spring the beauty is unsurpassed. It is a wonderful place to retreat and meditate by deep blue waters and lush green mountains. But in Jesus' day the shores were busy and bustling with fishing boats, not simple villages, but booming business areas where Jesus preached (Matt. 11:20-24).

As cool air from upland funnels and rushes down the gorges with great violence, the sea's position makes it liable for sudden storms. Such is frequent; thus, fishermen must be constantly alert and seldom venture far from shore. Some such storms are like hurricanes, and yet they are gone in less than ten minutes.

Many varieties of fish inhabit the sea. The industry in Jesus' day was pursued with profit. Zebedee even hired men to help him (Mark 1:20). 4 of the apostles were fishermen here: Peter, Andrew, James, and John. Most of the towns in Jesus' day around the western side of the lake were Jewish except Tiberias.

5 miles below the Sea of Galilee the Yarmuk River from Trans-Jordan and the mountains of Gilead meets the Jordan and again forms a delta. Below here the Valley of Jezreel empties into the Jordan at Beth-shean. The Ghor Valley contains the narrow Zor which carries the Jordan's flow still further south and is about 10-12 miles wide. Sedimentary lines on the Ghor mountains (either side) show possible water heights to about 650 feet up the mountain. The Jordan today only averages about 100 feet in width (except when spring flooding causes it to overflow a much wider area called the Zor). Some explorers find as many as 60 fords of the Jordan between the Sea of Galilee and the Dead Sea (all of

them are impassable during spring flooding). The Romans built the first bridges.

After passing the plain of Jericho on its right, the water empties into the Dead Sea. The Dead Sea's surface is 1,300 feet below sea level, and its bottom is about 2,600 feet below sea level. The sea is 50 miles long and from 10-15 miles wide.

Biblical References

The Lake of Gennesaret — *"And it came to pass, that, as the people pressed upon him to hear the word of God, he stood by the lake of Gennesaret"* (Luke 5:1).

"And when they were gone over, they came into the land of Gennesaret" (Matt. 14:34).

The Sea of Tiberias — *"After these things Jesus went over the sea of Galilee, which is the sea of Tiberias"* (John 6:1).

"After these things Jesus shewed himself again to the disciples at the sea of Tiberias; and on this wise shewed he himself" (John 21:1).

The Sea of Chinnereth — *"And the coast shall go down from Shephem to Riblah, on the east side of Ain; and the border shall descend, and shall reach unto the side of the sea of Chinnereth eastward"* (Num. 34:11).

The Sea of Galilee — *"And Jesus, walking by the sea of Galilee, saw two brethren, Simon called Peter, and Andrew his brother casting a net into the sea: for they were fishers"* (Matt. 4:18).

"And Jesus departed from thence, and came nigh unto the sea of Galilee; and went up into a mountain, and sat down there" (Matt. 15:29).

Much of Christ's earthly ministry was carried on in and around the Sea of Galilee — *"And leaving Nazareth, he came and dwelt in Capernaum, which is upon the sea coast, in the borders of Zabulon and Nephthalim: That it might be fulfilled which was spoken by Esaias the prophet, saying, The land of Zabulon, and the land of Nephtalim, by the of the sea, beyond Jordan, Galilee of the Gentiles; The people which sat in darkness saw great light; and to them which sat in the region and shadow of death light is sprung up"* (Matt. 4:13-16).

Peter and Andrew were called by Christ to be fishers of men, while they were fishing there — *"And Jesus, walking by the sea of Galilee, saw two brethren, Simon called Peter, and Andrew his brother, casting a net into the sea: for they were fishers. And he saith unto them, Follow me, and I will make you fishers of men. And they straighway left their nets, and followed him"* (Matt. 4:18-20).

James and John, while fishing in the Sea of Galilee were called by Christ to follow Him — *"And going on from thence, he saw two other brethren, James the son of Zebedee, and John his brother, in a ship with Zebedee their father, mending their nets; and he called them. And they immediately left the ship and their father, and followed him"* (Matt. 4:21-22).

The Sea of Galilee is noted for its sudden storms. It was on this lake, during one of those storms, when the disciples thought their boat would sink. Christ was asleep in the rear of the boat. When the disciples awakened Him and cried, "Carest thou not that we perish?" He stood and rebuked the storm with His "Peace, be still." Jesus sent the storm home, and put the sea to bed — *"And when they had sent away the multitude, they took him even as he was in the ship. And there were also with him other little ships. And there arose a great storm of wind, and the waves beat into the ship, so that it was now full. And he was in the hinder part of the ship, asleep on a pillow: and they awake him, and say unto him, Master, carest thou not that we perish? And he arose, and rebuked the wind, and said unto the sea, Peace, be still. And the wind ceased, and there was a great calm"* (Mark 4:36-39).

It was on this very sea Christ walked on the water — *"And when he had sent the multitudes away, he went up into a mountain apart to pray: and when the evening was come, he was there alone. But the ship was now in the midst of the sea, tossed with waves: for the wind was contrary. And in the fourth watch of the night Jesus went unto them, walking on the sea"* (Matt. 14:23-25).

It was also on the Sea of Galilee that Peter, at Christ's command, walked on the water — *"And when the disciples saw him walking on the sea, they were troubled, saying, It is a spirit; and they cried out for fear. But straightway Jesus spake unto them, saying, Be of good cheer; it is I, be not afraid. And Peter answered him and said, Lord if it be thou, bid me come unto thee on the water. And he said, Come. And when Peter was come down out of the ship, he walked on the water, to go to Jesus"* (Matt. 14:26-29).

At one time, 9 cities with a population of 15,000 or more stood on Galilee's shores. To the northwest was Capernaum, the home of Peter and Andrew, where Peter's mother-in-law was healed — *"And forthwith, when they were come out of the synagogue, they entered into the house of Simon and Andrew, with James and John. But Simon's wife's mother lay sick of a fever, and anon they tell him of her. And he came and took her by the hand, and lifted her up; and immediately the fever left her, and she ministered unto them"* (Mark 1:29-31).

Matthew sat at customs here in Capernaum, on the shore of Galilee — *"And as Jesus passed forth from thence, he saw a man, named Matthew, sitting at the receipt of custom: and he saith unto him, Follow me. And he arose, and followed him"* (Matt. 9:9).

Mary Magdalene's house was on the Sea of Galilee. It is on the western side at the Tower of Magdala — *"And he took the seven loaves and the fishes, and gave thanks, and brake them, and gave to his disciples, and the disciples to the multitude. And they did all eat, and were filled: and they took up of the broken meat that was left seven baskets full. And they that did eat were four thousand men, beside women and children. And he sent away the multitude and took ship, and came into the coasts of Magdala"* (Matt. 15:36-39).

"And certain women, which had been healed of evil spirits and infirmities, Mary called Magdalene, out whom went seven devils" (Luke 8:2).

Biblical Cities

Acre

Also known as Acco in the Old Testament and Ptolemais in the New Testament. Acre is located on the old Syrian coast north of Mt. Carmel and across the bay. This bay is the best harbor south of Beirut, Lebanon (thus is used by the Israeli navy). Acco commanded the approach to the Plain of Esdraelon and the northern coastal route, thus the city was of great importance as struggles for its possession point out. It was given to the tribe of Asher, but they could never conquer it (Josh. 19:24-31). The Phoenicians won it from Egypt in the twelfth century B.C. Assyria took it, but rebellion under Sennacharib and later Asshurbanipal brought wholesale massacre and captivity to the city. Later Babylon, then Persia possessed it. In New Testament days, it was called Ptolemais. Here Paul dwelt one day with "the brethren" (Acts 21:7).

Beersheba

The name means "seven wells" or "well of the oath." The city played an important part in the life of Israel's first patriarchs. Near here they camped and pastured their herds (Gen. 21:31). Abram and Abimelech took an oath of witness concerning Abram's digging of the well. Beersheba was a sacred shrine (Gen. 21:33), for here Abraham planted tamarisk trees. God appeared to Hagar (21:17), to Isaac (Gen. 26:24), to Jacob (Gen. 46:2), and later to Elijah (1 Kings 19:5) in Beersheba. Samuel's unworthy sons were judges here (1 Sam. 8:2), and King Joash's mother was born here (2 Kings 12:1). Beersheba marked Judah's southern limit. It was the border of civilized land. The statement of the nation's borders was "from Dan to Beersheba" (1 Chron. 22;2; 2 Chron. 30:5; 2 Sam. 17:11).

Bethlehem

The meaning of the name is not certain. It is generally thought to mean "house" or "place of bread," but there are 2 or 3 other possibilities. In Genesis 35:19 it is called Ephrath. It is also called the City of David, being his birthplace. Today the town is called Beit Lahm meaning "house of meat" in Arabic. It lies 5 miles south of Jerusalem. It lies in a position of natural strength and was a Philistine garrison in David's day (2 Sam. 23:14). It was later fortified by Rehoboam (2 Chron. 11:6). The countryside nearby is very fertile with fig trees, olive trees, and vineyards. Bethlehem has a natural spring and an aqueduct from one of Solomon's pools

In A.D. 132 the Roman Emperor Hadrian completely destroyed the city and afterward planted a grove sacred to a Roman god and goddess at the spot. He may have done this because it had become a place for religious pilgrimages concerning the birthplace of Jesus. Justin Martyr, about the year A.D. 150, mentions the birthplace of Jesus as a cave near the city. The best information is that from the time of Hadrian's destruction until about A.D. 325 the site lay desolate. In that year Helena, the mother of Constantine, had a basilica built in the area called the Church of the

Nativity. Shortly thereafter, in the time of Jerome, a cave near the church was venerated as the place of Jesus' birth. It is interesting to note also that in one of these nearby caves Jerome prepared his translation of the Bible known as the Vulgate. The building erected in the time of Constantine was damaged by fire in the Samaritan revolt. It was rebuilt under the Emperor Justanian about A.D. 550. Persian soldiers are said to have destroyed this church except for a fresco of the wisemen with Jesus painted on its inside wall. The magi wore Persian garments and the soldiers spared the Church of the Nativity. Other than modifications made during the Middle Ages, the building located here today is the one built by Justanian.

Biblical References

Rachel, Joseph's wife, was buried here — *"And they journeyed from Bethel; and there was but a little way to come to Ephrath: and Rachel travailed and she had hard labour. And it came to pass, when she was in hard labour, that the midwife said unto her, Fear not; thou shalt have this son also. And it came to pass, as her soul was departing, (for she died) that she called his name Benoni: but his father called him Benjamin. And Rachel died, and was buried in the way to Ephrath, which is Bethlehem. And Jacob set a pillar upon her grave: that is the pillar of Rachel's grave unto this day"* (Gen. 35:16-20).

Bethlehem was the home of Elimelech, the father-in-law of Ruth — *"Now it came to pass in the days when the judges ruled, that there was a famine in the land. And a certain man of Bethlehem-Judah went to sojourn in the country of Moab, he, and his wife, and his two sons. And the name of the man was Elimelech, and the name of his wife Naomi, and the name of his two sons Mahlon and Chilion, Ephrathites of Bethlehem-Judah. And they came into the country of Moab, and continued there"* (Ruth 1:1-2).

Boaz, Ruth's husband, lived there — *"And Noami had a kinsmen of her husband's, a mighty man of wealth, of the family of Elimelech; and his name was Boaz. And Ruth the Moabitess said unto Naomi, Let me now go to the field, and glean ears of corn after him in whose sight I shall find grace. And she said unto her, Go, my daughter. And she went, and came, and gleaned in the field after the reapers; and her hap was to light on a part of the field belonging unto Boaz, who was of the kindred of Elimelech. And, behold, Boaz came from Bethlehem, and said unto the reapers, The Lord be with you. And they answered him, The Lord bless thee"* (Ruth 2:1-4).

Ruth and Boaz's great grandson, David, kept his father's sheep here, and also was annointed king by Samuel here — *"Now David was the son of that Ephrathite of Bethlehem-Judah, whose name was Jesse; and he had eight sons: and the man went among men for a old man in the days of Saul. But David went and returned from Saul to feed his father's sheep at Bethlehem"* (1 Sam. 17:12, 15).

Jesus was born here — *"Now when Jesus was born in Bethlehem of Judea in the days of Herod the king, behold, there came wise men from the east to Jerusalem"* (Matt. 2:1).

"And Joseph also went up from Galilee, out of the city of Nazareth, into Judea, unto the city of David, which is called Bethlehem; (because he was of the house and lineage of David:) To be taxed with Mary his espoused wife, being great with child. And so it was, that, while they were there, the days were accomplished that she should be delivered. And she brought forth her firstborn son, and wrapped him in swaddling clothes, and laid him in a manger; because there was no room for them in the inn" (Luke 2:4-7).

It was in Bethlehem that all the male children 2 years of age and under were ordered killed by Herod — *"Then Herod, when he saw that he was mocked of the wise men, was exceeding wroth, and sent forth, and slew all the children that were in Bethlehem, and in all the coasts thereof, from two years old and under, according to the time which he had diligently enquired of the wise men"* (Matt. 2:16).

The shepherds went here the night of Christ's birth to

see what glorious thing had happened — *And it came to pass, as the angels were gone away from them into heaven, the shepherds said one to another, Let us now go even unto Bethlehem, and see this thing which is come to pass, which the Lord hath made known unto us. And they came with haste, and found Mary, and Joseph, and the babe lying in a manger"* (Luke 2:15-16).

70 — *Israel and the Holy Land*

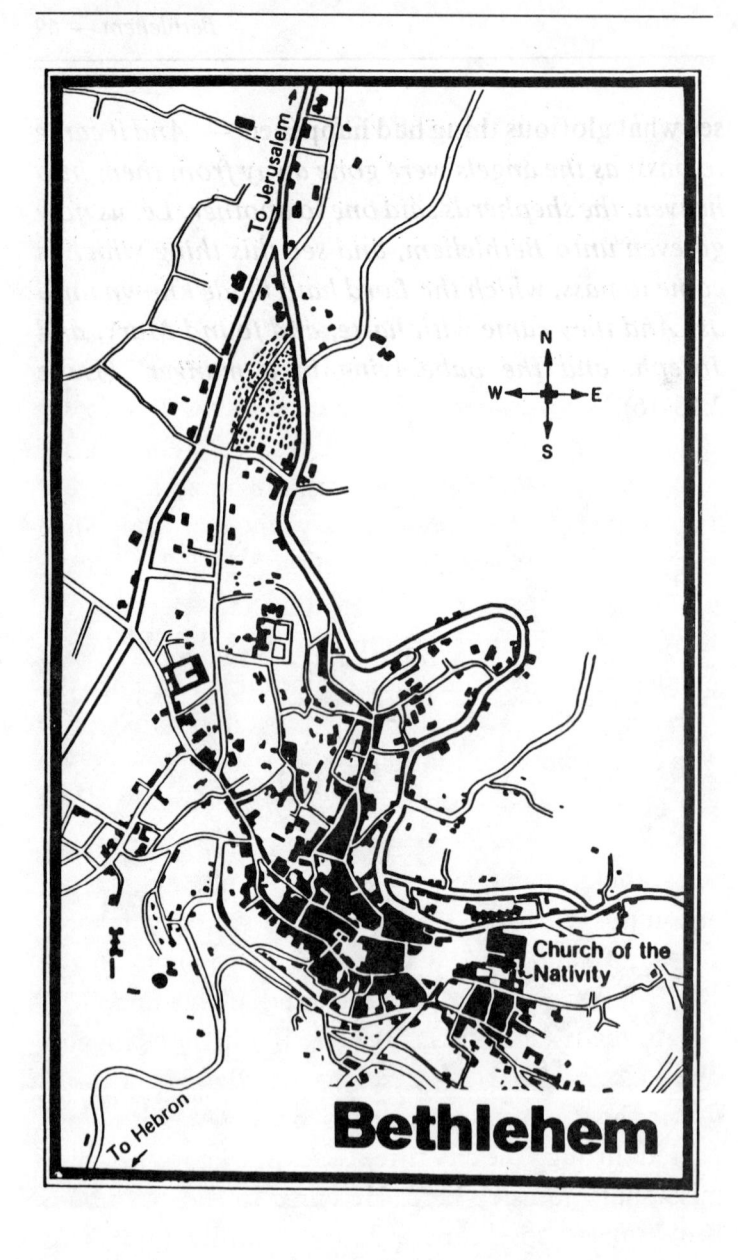

Caesarea

The city is located 30 miles north of Jaffa and 27 miles northwest of Jerusalem. It was built in 22 B.C. by Herod the Great on the site of the Old Testament Strato's Tower and named Caesarea Sebate after Augustus Caesar. It remained the Roman capital of Palestine for approximately 500 years. Herod lavished adornments on the city, erecting palaces, public buildings, a theater, and an amphitheater. It was Herod's main connecting link with Rome. It had a magnificent harbor. It was a remarkable feat since the whole area was not at all suited for such construction. The breakwater was built by letting stones 50 x 18 x 9 feet to some 20 fathoms depth. The foundation was 200 feet wide and on top were walls and a tower. A city for trade and mariners was built. And this was all accomplished in 10-12 years. Here the Roman procurator Pilate lived. It's referred to 15 times in the Book of Acts. It came into the hand of Agrippa I and here he died (Acts 12:19, 23). Here Philip the evangelist dwelt (Acts 8:40; 21:8). Peter was sent here from Jaffa to win the Roman centurion Cornelius (Acts 10). Paul passed through the city three times and ended his third missionary journey here. He came to the city under heavy guard to escape a Jewish murder plot. This city's prison was his home for two years while he waited to come to trial.

A quarrel here in A.D. 66 between the Jews and the Greeks led to the Jewish revolt. During this time, Caesarea was the headquarters for the Roman legion. They tortured the Jews horribly in punishment for their rebellion. Here Vespasian was hailed emperor by his soldiers. Here Titus celebrated his brother's birthday by placing 2,500 Jews in the amphitheater to fight wild beasts. After the revolt, Caesarea became a Gentile city with a large Jewish population.

Biblical References

Philip the evangelist stopped at Caesarea at the close of his preaching tour — *"But Philip was found at Azotus: and passing through he preached in all the cities, till he came to Caesarea"* (Acts 8:40).

Paul was brought here by the brethren and sent by ship to Tarsus after the Hellenists determined to kill him — *"Which when the brethren knew, they brought him down to Caesarea, and sent him forth to Tarsus"* (Acts 9:30).

The Roman centurion Cornelius had his vision of the angel who instructed him to send for Peter here — *"There was a certain man in Caesarea called Cornelius, a centurion of the band called the Italian band . . . He saw in a vision . . . an angel of God coming in to* him . . . *And he said unto him . . . Send men to Joppa, and call for one Simon, whose surname is Peter"* (Acts 10:1-5).

Peter had his vision of the sheet filled with animals descending from Heaven on the rooftop in Caesarea — *". . . Peter went up upon the housetop to pray about the sixth hour . . . And saw heaven opened, and a certain vessel descending unto him, as it had been a great sheet knit at the four corners, and let down to the earth: Wherein were all manner of fourfooted beasts of the earth, and wild beasts, and creeping things, and fowls of the air . . . This was done thrice: and the vessel was received up again into heaven"* (Acts 10:9-16).

At the close of his second missionary journey Paul landed at Caesarea and greeted the church. He later took up residence here with Philip — *"And the next day we that were of Paul's company departed, and came unto Caesarea: and we entered into the house of Philip the evangelist, which was one of the seven; and abode with him"* (Acts 21:8).

After his arrest in Jerusalem Paul was taken to Felix the governor in Caesarea — *"Then the soldiers, as it was commanded them, took Paul, and brought him by night to Antipatris. Who, when they came to Caesarea, and delivered the epistle* [Felix], *presented Paul also before him"* (Acts 23:31, 33).

Here Paul was imprisoned in Herod's judgment hall — *"I will hear thee, said he, when thine accusers are also come. And he commanded him to be kept in Herod's judgment hall"* (Acts 23:35).

Capernaum

Capernaum was on the western shore of the Sea of Galilee. If recent discoveries are to be trusted, it was of sufficient importance to give to that sea in whole or in part the name of the "Lake of Capernaum." It was of sufficient size to always be called a "city." Capernaum had its own synagogue in which our Lord frequently taught.

Woe was spoken against this city by Jesus (Matt. 11:23; Luke 10:15). Capernaum was the headquarters of Jesus' Galilean ministry (Matt. 4:13). Near here He called the fishermen to follow Him (Mark 1:16), as well as the publican (tax collector) Levi, later called Matthew (Matt. 9:9). It was the scene of His "mighty works" (Matt. 11:23; Mark 1:34). Here Jesus healed the nobleman's son (John 4:46), Peter's mother-in-law (Mark 1:31), the paralytic (Matt. 1:1), cast out the unclean spirits (Mark 1:23), and raised Jairus' daughter to life (Mark 5:22). Here a little child was used to teach the disciples humility, and in the synagogue Jesus delivered His discourse on the "bread of life" (John 6).

It may have once stood on considerable importance (Matt. 11:23; Luke 10:15) or may have been the excessive pride of the inhabitants that is mentioned. It was a customs station and a residence of a high officer of the king (Matt. 9:9; John 4:46). Here resided a detachment of Roman soldiers who even helped to construct a synagogue for the Jews to get their good will (Matt. 8:5; Luke 7:5). It stood by the "Sea" (Matt. 4:13), and was near the Plain of Gennesaret (John 6:17; Matt. 14:34; Mark 6:53).

In the Old Testament, Joshua mentiones Capernaum, but it was not prominent then. It may have been the home of Nahum the prophet.

It is located at the north end of the sea on an important highway to North Trans-Jordan, thus, its customs house and military guards.

Biblical References

Jesus dwelt in Capernaum — *"And leaving Nazareth, he came and dwelt in Capernaum, which is upon the sea coast, in the borders of Zabulon and Nephthalim"* (Matt. 4:13).

Jesus healed the centurion's servant in Capernaum — *"And when Jesus was entered in Capernaum, there came unto him a centurion, beseeching him. And saying, Lord, my servant lieth at home sick of the palsy, grievously tormented. And Jesus saith unto him, I will come and heal him"* (Matt. 8:5-7).

Jesus healed Peter's mother-in-law in Capernaum — *"And when Jesus was come into Peter's house, he saw his wife's mother laid, and sick of a fever. And he touched her hand, and the fever left her and she arose, and ministered unto them"* (Matt. 8:14-15).

Capernaum was an exalted city until Jesus had to upbraid them for their failure to repent — *"And thou Capernaum, which art exalted unto heaven, shalt be brought down to hell; for if the mighty works, which have been done in thee, had been done in Sodom, it would have remained until this day. But I say unto you, That it shall be more tolerable for the land of Sodom in the day of judgment than for thee"* (Matt. 11:23-24).

Jesus taught on the Sabbath day at Capernaum — *"And came down to Capernaum, a city of Galilee, and taught them on the sabbath day"* (Luke 4:31).

Jesus healed the man with the unclean spirit at Capernaum — *"And in the synagogue there was a man, which had a spirit of an unclean devil, and cried out with a loud voice. Saying, Let us alone; what have we to do with thee, thou Jesus of Nazareth? are thou come to destroy us? I know thee who thou art; the Holy One of God. And Jesus rebuked him, saying, Hold thy peace, and come out of him. And when the devil had thrown him in the midst, he came out of him, and hurt him not"* (Luke 4:33-35).

The disciples were off the shore of **Capernaum** when Jesus walked on the water — *"And entered into a ship,* *and went over the sea toward Capernaum. And it was now dark, and Jesus was not come to them. And the sea arose by reason of a great wind that blew. So when they had rowed about five and twenty or thirty furlongs, they saw Jesus walking on the sea, and drawing nigh unto the ship: and they were afraid"* (John 6:17-19).

Jesus taught in the synagogue at Capernaum — *"These things said he in the synagogue, as he taught in Capernaum"* (John 6:59).

Jericho

Ancient Jericho is called Tell-es-Sultan and lies very near Elisha's Fountain (2 Kings 2:19-23) which Elisha sweetened by throwing a cruse of salt into it. Even today it gives a copious, never-failing water supply for the entire area and is even used for irrigation in Jericho.

Ancient Jericho is a mound made up entirely of accumulated debris of human occupation. During the past 50 years, extensive excavations have taken place. The discoveries have been fabulous. The site dates back as far as 8000 B.C. when the first fishers and hunters settled by the copious spring. From this period has been found a defense tower built before 7000 B.C. (or 4,000 years before the Pyramids of Egypt were built). Human skulls from the ruins date to about 4500 B.C.; finely-built Neolithic homes have been dated from 6000-4500 B.C.; and mud-brick town walls of the Early Bronze age from 3000-2000 B.C.. Many tombs of the Hyksos or Middle Bronze age have been found. The topmost wall dated about 1400 B.C.. Thus, the Tell dates from about 8000-1700 B.C.

From the ruins of Jericho archaeologists deduce these facts: By 7000 B.C. the Neolithic man was leading a communal life and erected walls for protection.

They built elaborate towers, yet only flint and stone tools were available as metal had not been discovered (this date was even prior to pottery making). Agriculture was practiced and bread was made. The homes were plastered on the inside and figurines were molded in clay. The pre-pottery Neolithic man inhabited Jericho for many years and was followed by the pottery making Neolithic man. They had public buildings, stronger walls, and made tools of flint, but none of their skeletons remain. However, lifesize statues have been found. This period ended about 4000 B.C. and the succeeding culture was Chalcolithic, who introduced metal. The Chalcolithic people dwelt there until about 3200 B.C.. One tomb from this period held 113 skulls and a pile of burnt bones in the center which was a form of cremation.

The next age was Early Bronze from 2900-2300 B.C. with city defenses that were remarkable. The walls were rebuilt about 16 times within a period of 600 years. Finally, the city was invaded by nomads who built temples and made dull pottery (strictly utilitarian). These people were probably Amorites who overran the Middle East about 2300-1900 B.C. They brought with them a higher culture and the use of the potter's wheel (the Middle Bronze age) The Hyksos, or Shepherd Kings of the Bible set up new defenses and came to use the horse (maybe even chariots in Palestine and Egypt). Thus, new defenses were built at Jericho to protect from such invasions.

The Iron age followed (being the age of Joshua).

Little of this city remains (not even tombs from this period). There are a few remains of the walls (which fell to the outside). Since this era ended the period of Old Testament Tell-es-Sultan, the erosion of the top of the Tell has not helped to preserve it for our present-day knowledge. The mound measures 1,200 feet by 60 feet high. Where archaeology has to leave off, the Old Tesament and New Testament records fill in much of the city's history.

In Deuteronomy 32:49 and 34:3, its location is mentioned and it is called a city of palm trees. Joshua tells of its walls (Josh. 2:15), its gates (Josh. 2:5), and its king. There, after the capture, they found Babylonian garments, gold, and silver (Josh. 7:21). It lay across the Jordan from the Israel camp Shittim (Josh. 2:1), in the plain (Josh. 4:13), close to the mountains. Here the spies found Rahab. It was later allotted to Benjamin (Josh. 18:21). The city was rebuilt (1 Kings 16:34) by Hiel in Ahab's day and Joshua's earlier curse (Josh. 6:26) was then fulfilled. David's messengers tarried there (2 Sam. 10:15) and in Elisha's day a school for prophets was founded there (2 Kings 2:5).

In Jesus' day Herod had rebuilt the city and to this city pilgrims first came from crossing the Jordan at its fords (as they traveled from Galilee to Jerusalem, and of course, avoided Samaria). Here Jesus healed blind Bartimaeus (Matt. 20:29-34; Mark 10:46-52; Luke 18:35-43), and encountered Zacchaeus (Luke 19:1-28). Beyond this city He often took His disciples for instruction. On one such occasion He was told of

Lazarus' death in Bethany (John 11:1-4). Just north of Jericho He was tempted in the wilderness.

Biblical References

The land inheritance of Reuben, Gad, and the half-tribe of Manasseh lay near Jericho — *"The two tribes and the half tribe have received their inheritance on this side Jordan near Jericho eastward, toward the sunrising"* (Num. 34:15).

Moses viewed the promised land from Mt. Nebo, which lay in the land of Moab, against Jericho — *"Get thee up into this mountain Abram, unto mount Nebo, which is in the land of Moab, that is over against Jericho; and behold the land of Canaan, which I give unto the children of Israel for a possession"* (Deut. 32:49).

Joshua sent two spies to view the promised land, including Jericho — *"And Joshua the son of Nun sent out of Shittim two men to spy secretly, saying, Go view the land, even Jericho"* (Josh. 2:1).

The harlot, Rahab, hid the two spies on her rooftop, and afterward let them down by a cord through the window — *"And they went, and came into an harlot's house, named Rahab, and lodged there . . . And the woman took the two men, and hid them, and said thus, There came men unto me, but I wist not whence they were . . . Then she let them down by a cord through the window: for her house was upon the town wall, and she dwelt upon the wall"* (Josh. 2).

Elisha and Elijah passed through Jericho on their way to the place where God would take Elijah home in a fiery chariot — *"And Elijah said unto him, Elisha, tarry here, I pray thee; for the Lord hath sent me to Jericho. And he said, As the Lord liveth, and as thy soul liveth, I will not leave thee. So they came to Jericho"* (2 Kings 2:4).

The men of Jericho assisted Nehemiah in the rebuilding of the wall of Jerusalem — *"And next unto him builded the men of Jericho"* (Neh. 3:2).

Jesus ministered to the Jews in Jericho — *"And as they departed from Jericho, a great multitude followed him"* (Matt. 20:29).

Jesus healed blind Bartimaeus on the highway outside the city of Jericho — *"And they came to Jericho: and as he went out of Jericho with his disciples and a great number of people, blind Bartimaeus, the son of Timaeus, sat by the highway side begging . . . And he began to cry out, and say, Jesus . . . have mercy on me . . . And Jesus said unto him, Go thy way; thy faith hath made thee whole"* (Mark 10:46-52).

Jesus used the city of Jericho in His parable of the

good Samaritan — *"And Jesus answering said, A certain man went down from Jerusalem to Jericho, and fell among thieves . . ."* (Luke 10:30).

The well-known Zacchaeus who climbed the sycamore tree was a native of Jericho — *"And Jesus entered and passed through Jericho. And, behold, there was a man named Zacchaeus, which was the chief among the publicans, and he was rich"* (Luke 19:1-2).

The city of Jericho is included in the great faith chapter, Hebrews 11.

Jerusalem

The earliest mention of Jerusalem was 1450 B.C. In the Tell-Amarna cuneiform letters as Urasalim and in the eighth century B.C. on an Assyrian monument as Ursaliimmu. The most ancient biblical form is Yerushalem (Ps. 76:2), where it's shortened to Salem.

In the New Testament we have Hierousalem and in A.D. 1611 in the King James as Ierosalem (O.T.) and Hisrusalem (N.T.) The original name probably meant "City of Peace," "Possession of Peace," or "Foundation of Peace." An irony of history is that the city's long history has seen little peace and rivers of blood have been shed for its possession.

Other names of the city are: Jebus, "City of Righteousness"; and in Philo's day, Hieropolis, "The Holy City."

Jerusalem is built on formations of limestone, with strata containing flint. There is no primary rock, no sandstone, and no volcanic rock. The formations are in a regular strata and dip toward the southeast at about 10 degrees.

The climate is very healthy. The winter's cold is severely felt for it coincides with the heaviest rains (Ezra 10:9). The lowest recorded temperature is 25 degrees fahrenheit, with maybe a dozen nights a year with frost. During the rainless summer months, the temperature climbs to 74 degrees by August and in September the temperature often hits 100 degrees in the shade, but cool northwestern breezes blow during the early evening hours. The most unpleasant days occur in May and from mid-September through October when dry southeast winds blow in desert heat and dust ("humsen"). During the late summer, heavy dews occur at night and at the end of September or the beginning of October the "former rains" begin in tropical downpours. This is followed by several dry weeks, then the "winter rains" fall in December, January, and February (and in some areas of Palestine as late as March). The average Jerusalem rainfall is 25 inches. Some winter seasons snow falls heavily on Jerusalem.

Only one actual spring is found in the area (Gihon in the Old Testament and today called The Virgin's Fountain). It lies in a rocky cleft in the Kidron Valley. A wall was built to bank the water into pools and in 2 Chronicles 32:4, Hezekiah constructed a tunnel for its flow. Thus, he brought the water supply inside the city wall and prevented enemies from getting the water. The water empties into the Pool of Siloam channeled by Hezekiah's Tunnel or Siloam Tunnel.

Probably the earliest dwellers lived in caves near this water supply (2000 B.C.). The Canaanites built a 67 foot aquaduct from Gihon (2000-1500 B.C.). It is probably the "watercourse" in 2 Samuel 5:8 and

1 Chronicles 11:6. By David's time it may have been 1,000 years old. Hezekiah's Siloam aqueduct branches off from the former and travels 1,749 feet (a little over a quarter of a mile) to the Pool of Siloam. The canal is rock cut 2-3 feet wide and is from 16-4½ feet high. The Siloam inscription found in the mid-point of the canal tells of its construction. It was begun simultaneously in 700 B.C. from each end and then the 2 parties met in the middle beneath Mt. Ophel (2 Kings 20:20). Hezekiah had the matter accomplished in great haste before Sennacherib's advancing army arrived at the Jerusalem walls. Above the tunnel stood Solomon's Temple. Though the tunnel is 1,749 feet long, a direct measurement from the 2 points is 1,098 feet.

Other references to the Pool of Siloam or Shiloah are found in Nehemiah 3:15; Isaiah 8:6; John 9:1-11. References to Gihon are found in 1 Kings 1:33, 38, 45; 2 Chronicles 32:4, 30; 33:14; Nehemiah 2:13-15; 3:13-16; Isaiah 7:3; 22:9-11; 36:2). The Sheep Pool of John 5:2 is a large reservoir consisting of twin pools totalling 125 feet in length. Many believe it to be the Pool of Bethesda (John 5:2-4) of Jesus' day (found near the Sheep Gate and the Temple area). Pontius Pilate built a long aqueduct from Solomon's Pools of Bethlehem to Jerusalem. Today, Jerusalem's Arab side gets its water from near Anathoth and the Israel side from Ras el-'Ain in the Plain of Sharon. Today as in Bible days, water shortage is always a danger to Jerusalem's residents.

Jerusalem lies in the midst of a bare and rocky

plateau, one of the least fruitful areas of Palestine. The city itself stands where 3 steep-sided little wadis gather together to form one valley. They are the Kidron Valley, the Tyropoeon Valley, and the Valley of Hinnom. Between the Kidron and Tyropoeon valleys a long, narrow spur extends southward, and it was on this narrow spur that the first town was built, the town of Jebus. This was the town which was taken by David and which he made into his capital. It is very strongly defended by steep descents on all sides except the north, where it is joined to the main plateau. When David captured it, the level land on top of the spur must have been thickly covered with houses, for it is a very small area. He therefore started a process of building out northward, and it was on that side that he built his palace and bought the land on which the Temple was later to be erected. This was the threshing floor of Araunah the Jebusite (2 Sam. 24:18). The city remained roughly like this until the time of the captivity, though it must have continued to spread out rather farther to the north and west, for Zephaniah speaks of "the inhabitants of the Mortar" (Zeph. 1:11), which suggests that the hollow formed by the Tyropoeon Valley had been at any rate partly included, for the word is used elsewhere for a hollow place (Jud. 15:19). This is the picture of the city given in Psalm 48:2:

> *"Beautiful for situation, the joy of the whole earth, is mount Zion, on the sides of the north,*

the city of the great King."

It is by no means the highest part of the plateau, but is surrounded with higher land, the "mountains that are round about Jerusalem" (Ps. 125:2); there is no need, therefore, to equate Jerusalem with "a city set on a hill" (Matt. 5:14), as is often done.

By New Testament days, the extension of the north and west had proceeded much farther, and the whole of the western hill between the Tyropoeon Valley and the Valley of Hinnom had been included. Tyropoeon Valley was then much lower than it is at present, for it has gradually been filled up with rubble during the centuries. In later Roman times the city extended far to the north of the present medieval walls, which were built by Suleiman the Magnificent in the sixteenth century A.D.. These surround what is known today as the Old City, which includes the area of the ancient Temple and its southeastern corner. Until the middle of the nineteenth century no building was allowed outside the walls, but since that date the city has grown greatly, always to the north and west, leaving entirely outside it the most ancient part of all, the town of Jebus.

The existing walls go back to A.D. 1542, but they oftentimes are built over previous walls much more ancient. The modern wall is 2⅛ miles long and an average of 35 feet high. It has 35 towers and 8 gates. The present wall is a patchwork of many periods of history. The development of the walls is too involved for us to enter the study presently. Your map points out a few matters concerning them. The most complete scriptural description of them is given in Nehemiah. Even in his day traces of the oldest wall remained, and he sought to restore the same (Neh. 2:13-51; 3:1-32; 12:31-39). These verses mention the Valley Gate; Dung Gate; Fountain Gate; Water Gate; Horse Gate; Sheep Gate (also Zech. 14:10); Fish Gate (Zeph. 1:10; 2 Chron. 33:14), and probably "the Middle Gate of Jerusalem"; the Old Gate or Corner Gate (2 Kings 14:13; 2 Chron. 25:23; Jer. 31:38; Zech. 14:10); Gate of Ephraim (2 Kings 14:13; 2 Chron. 25:23); Gate of Benjamin (Jer. 20:2; 37:13; 38:7; Zech. 14:10; and the Upper Gate of the Temple (2 Kings 15:35; 2 Chron. 37:3; 23:20; Ezek. 9:2). Solomon was probably the first to enclose the northern and western stretches of the "First Wall." David before him had been protected by the powerful fortifications of the Jebusites which enclosed the southeastern area of the hill. David added the defenses of the fortress Millo. At that time the Jebusite city probably had only one city gate to the north. As the city grew, Solomon increased its length in the northern direction and there built his capital and the Temple. According to the Jewish Talmud:

> "When the world was created, it received ten measures of beauty. Nine fell on Jerusalem . . . one on the rest of the earth."

It is one of the most famous cities on earth and is

sacred to Christians, Jews, and Muslims.

Some Basic Facts About Modern Jerusalem

1. *Population* — About 365,000
2. *Area* — 41 square miles
3. *Altitude* — 2,400 feet above sea level
4. *Average July Temperature* — 76 degrees fahrenheit
5. *Occupation* — In the Arab-Israeli war of 1948, Jerusalem was divided between Israel (West Jerusalem) and Jordan (East Jerusalem). Israel won East Jerusalem in the 1967 war and combined it with West Jerusalem.
6. *Religion* — West Jerusalem: Mostly Jewish, a few Christians and Muslims; East Jerusalem: Mostly Muslim, a few Catholics and Greek Orthodox

The Holy Places

1. *The Wailing Wall* — Also called the Western Wall, on Mt. Moriah, 160 feet long, was the western wall of the Herodian Temple courtyard. It has long been a symbol of Jewish faith and unity. It takes its name from the sorrowful prayers uttered there, mourning the destruction of the Temple.
2. *Church of the Holy Sepulchre* — This is the traditional site of the death and burial of Jesus, dating from the time of Constantine (fourth century A.D.), whose mother claimed to have had a vision, locating the spot (then occupied by a temple to

Venus). Constantine destroyed the pagan temple and erected Christian churches that have since been torn down and replaced by the present church. The site is located at the end of the Via Dolorosa (Way of Sorrows), traditionally the route which Jesus took when carrying His cross to Calvary. Some may question whether or not this site is outside the walls of Jerusalem, as Calvary was located, according to the gospel accounts. It is now known, however, that this site was indeed outside the then-existing walls of the city, although not outside of the present walls. It is not known certainly that this is indeed the site of the passion, however.

3. *Gordon's Calvary* — Popular optional site of the death of Jesus, just north of the traditional site and adjacent to the Garden Tomb. This site was brought to the attention of Christian pilgrims and scholars in 1883 by British General Charles Gordon, who noted a decided likeness of the site to a skull (Golgotha means "place of a skull"). He also found adjacent tombs which might correspond to the gospel accounts of the burial of Jesus in a nearby tomb. Failure to discover a wall of Jerusalem nearby, however, has led meny scholars to question the authenticity of the location. Its preserved natural simplicity, in contrast to the Church of the Holy Sepulchre, has greatly appealed to many Christian tourists, and even if it is not exactly the original site, it may well reflect rather accurately something of what that site was like.

4. *The Dome of the Rock* — A Muslim mosque (sometimes erroneously called the Mosque of Omar) located at the ancient site of the Jewish Temple. It is second only to Mecca as a sacred shrine for Muslims. According to Muslim traditions, the mosque was built over the rock from which Mohammed rose to heaven with the angel Gabriel and spoke with God. With God's blessing, Mohammed returned from his night's journey to spread Islam, the new religion. Jews believe that on this rock Abraham prepared to sacrifice Isaac (Gen. 22), i.e. Mt. Moriah.

Brief History of Jerusalem

1. First biblical reference was probably Salem of Genesis 14, ruled by the mysterious Melchizedek (Heb. 7) who was also "priest of the most high God," a notable type of Jesus Christ. This would indicate (liberal theology to the contrary notwithstanding) that there were worshippers to the one true God in that ancient area as early as ca. 2000 B.C., although we have no knowledge of such from other sources.
2. Probably to be identified with the "land of Moriah" (Gen. 22).
3. At the time of the conquest of Canaan, the Jews found the city in the hands of an indigenous Semitic tribe, the Jebusites (and known as Jebus), ruled by one Adonizedek, who formed an alliance of kings

against Joshua. Joshua soundly thrashed them but did not take the city, undoubtedly because of its strong geographical location (Josh. 10; Jud. 1:8, 21).

4. David captured the city (2 Sam. 5) and made it his capital, replacing Hebron. This was not only a brilliant tactical move, but also a smart political strategem. Jerusalem, on the Benjamin-Judah border would help to diminish the tribal jealousies between the two. The name Zion first appears here, apparently the name of the hill on which the Jebusite citadel stood.

5. Solomon carried to fruition David's desire to erect a permanent home for the ark of the covenant. The magnificent Solomon's Temple was the result — perhaps the most lavishly expensive building ever constructed.

6. After the division of the kingdom at the death of Solomon (c. 931 B.C.), his son Rehoboam suffered a plundering by Egyptian troops (1 Kings 14:25). Philistine and Arab marauders again plundered the Temple in Jehoram's reign. In Amaziah's reign, Northern Kingdom plunderers again struck the Temple, the palace, and partially destroyed the city wall. Uzziah repaired the damage.

7. Nebuchadnezzar and his neo-Babylonian troops destroyed the city and the Temple in 586 B.C. Much of the population was taken into captivity in Babylon. Jerusalem became a ruin, populated only by some of the poor and outcast people remaining.

8. Some 70 years later, the Jews, now under Persian rule, were permitted to return to their land and city. They rebuilt the Temple, led by Zerubbabel, but the city walls lay in ruins until Nehemiah restored them in the middle of the fifth century B.C.
9. During the Intertestamental Period, Israel (and Jerusalem) passed under the control of Greece (331-323 B.C.), Egypt (323-198 B.C.), and Syria (198-168 B.C.), before attaining a century of independence (168-63 B.C.) under Maccabean rule. Roman rule commenced in 63 B.C. with the conquest of Pompey.
10. Under Roman rule, Herod the Great made great improvements in the physical appearance of Jerusalem, the most notable project being the renovation (almost the rebuilding) of the second Temple. The so-called Herod's Temple is the structure which we know from the gospel narratives.
11. Jerusalem (including the Temple) was utterly destroyed in A.D. 70 by Roman legions under Titus. Perhaps as many as one million Jews were slain.
12. In A.D. 132 the Emperor Hadrian rebuilt Jerusalem (on a smaller scale) as a pagan city, dedicated to Jupiter Capitolinus. Jews were forbidden entrance until the time of Constantine (early fourth century A.D.). Jerusalem then became a Christian city with much building activity — including the original Church of the Holy Sepulchre.

13. Persians partially destroyed the city in A.D. 614. The Muslims arrived in A.D. 637, led by Caliph Omar, and Jerusalem became a Muslim city. The Dome of the Rock was constructed in A.D. 691.
14. Christian crusades captured Jerusalem in 1099, and it became a Christian city again — briefly.
15. Jerusalem was reconquered in 1187 and remained in Muslim hands until World War I. British General Allenby entered Jerusalem in 1917, and the city became a British mandate until 1948, when it was divided between Jews and Arabs.

Biblical Reference

Melchizedek, king of Salem, priest of the Most High, blesses Abraham after Abraham delivers Lot and his people from Chedorlaomer, king of Elam — *"And Melchizedek king of Salem brought forth bread and wine: and he was the priest of the most high God"* (Gen. 14:18).

Jerusalem was previously occupied by the Jebusites before Joshua led God's people to destroy them and take possession in the promised land — *"And the border went up by the valley of the son of Hinnom unto the south side of the Jebusite; the same is Jerusalem: and the border went up to the top of the mountain that lieth before the valley of Hinnom westward, which is at the end of the valley of the giants northward"* (Josh. 15:8).

Jebusi, which is Jerusalem along with 13 other cities with their villages, was the inheritance of the children of Benjamin — *"And Zelah, Eleph, and Jebusi, which is Jerusalem, Gibeath, and Kirjath; fourteen cities with their villages. This is the inheritance of the children of Benjamin according to their families"* (Josh. 18:28).

The children of Benjamin did not drive out the Jebusites but dwelled with them — *"And the children of Benjamin did not drive out the Jebusites that inhabited Jerusalem; but the Jebusites dwell with the children of Benjamin in Jerusalem unto this day"* (Jud. 1:21).

David cut off the head of Goliath and brought it back to Jerusalem — *"And David took the head of the Philistine, and brought it to Jerusalem; but he put his armour in his tent"* (1 Sam. 17:54).

The elders of Israel annointed David as king over Israel. King David and his army went to Jerusalem, the stronghold of Zion, to conquer the Jebusites who were still inhabiting the land. After capturing the city, he names it the "city of David" from where he ruled his kingdom — *"And the king and his men went to Jerusalem unto the Jebusites, the inhabitants of the land: which spake unto David, saying, Except thou take away the blind and the lame, thou shalt not come in hither: thinking, David cannot come in hither.*

Nevertheless David took the strong hold of Zion: the same is the city of David. And David said on that day, Whosoever getteth up to the gutter, and smiteth the Jebusites, and the lame and the blind, that are hated of David's soul, he shall be chief and captain. Wherefore they said, The blind and the lame shall not come into the house" (2 Sam. 5:6-8).

David has the ark of God moved to the tabernacle in Jerusalem — *"And it was told king David, saying, The Lord hath blessed the house of Obededom, and all that pertaineth unto him, because of the ark of God. So David went and brought up the ark of God from the house of Obededom into the city of David with gladness. And it was so, that when they that bare the ark of the Lord had gone six paces, he sacrificed oxen and fatlings. And David danced before the Lord with all his might; and David was girded with a linen ephod.df So David and all the house of Israel brought up the ark of the Lord with shouting, and with the sound of the trumpet. And as the ark of the Lord came into the city of David, Michal Saul's daughter looked through a window, and saw king David leaping and dancing before the Lord; and she despised him in her heart. And they brought in the ark of the Lord, and set it in his place, in the midst of the tabernacle that David had pitched for it: and David offered burnt offerings and peace offerings before the Lord"* (2 Sam. 6:12-17).

Solomon builds the Temple in Jerusalem. Hiram, king of Tyre, supplies the timber from the firs and cedars of Lebanon — *"And, behold, I purpose to build an house unto the name of the Lord my God, as the Lord spake unto David my father, saying, Thy son, whom I will set upon thy throne in thy room, he shall build an house unto my name. Now therefore command thou that they hew me cedar trees out of Lebanon; and my servants shall be with thy servants: and unto thee will I give hire for thy servants according to all that thou shalt appoint: for thou knowest that there is not among us any that can skill to hew timber like unto the Sidonians. And it came to pass, when Hiram heard the words of Solomon, that he rejoiced greatly, and said, Blessed be the Lord this day, which hath given unto David a wise son over this great people. And Hiram sent to Solomon, saying, I have considered the things which thou sentest to me for: and I will do all thy desire concerning timber of cedar, and concerning timber of fir"* (1 Kings 5:5-8).

Sennacherib, the king of Assyria, threatens King Hezekiah with destroying Jerusalem. As the armies are encamped around Jerusalem, the angel of the Lord smites 185,000 men of the Assyrian army. Jerusalem is protected — *"For out of Jerusalem shall go forth a remnant and they that escape out of mount Zion: the zeal of the Lord of hosts shall do this. Therefore thus saith the Lord concerning the king of Assyria, He shall not come into this city, nor shoot an arrow there, nor come before it with shield, nor cast a bank against it. By the way that he came, by the same shall he return, and shall not come into this city, saith the Lord. For I will defend this city, to save it, for mine own sake, and for my servant David's sake. And it came to pass that night, that the angel of the Lord went out, and smote in the camp of the Assyrians an hundred fourscore and five thousand: and when they arose early in the morning, behold, they were all dead corpses. So Sennacherib king of Assyria departed, and went and returned, and dwelt at Nineveh"* (2 Kings 19:31-36).

In the ninth year of Zedekiah, king of Judah in the tenth month, Jerusalem is beseiged by the army of King Nebuchadnezzar of Babylon — *"At that time the servants of Nebuchadnezzar king of Babylon came up against Jerusalem, and the city was besieged. And Nebuchadnezzar king of Babylon came against the city, and his servants did besiege it"* (2 Kings 24:10-11).

King Zedekiah's sons are slain before him, then his eyes were put out and he was bound with chains to be carried to Babylon — *"And in the eleventh year of Zedekiah, in the fourth month, the ninth day of the month, the city was broken up . . . Then the king of Babylon slew the sons of Zedekiah in Riblah before his eyes: also the king of Babylon slew all the nobles of Judah. Moreover he put out Zedekiah's eyes, and bound him with chains, to carry him to Babylon" (Jer. 39:2, 6-7).*

Jerusalem was desolate for 70 years and the people served the king of Babylon for 70 years — *"And this whole land shall be a desolation, and an astonishment; and these nations shall serve the king of Babylon seventy years. And it shall come to pass, when seventy years are accomplished, that I will punish the king of Babylon, and that nation, saith the Lord, for their iniquity, and the land of the Chaldeans, and will make it perpetual desoltions"* (Jer. 25:11-12).

Cyrus the king of Persia declares that he should build a house for God at Jerusalem — *"Now in the first year of Cyrus king of Persia, that the word of the Lord by the mouth of Jeremiah might be fulfilled, the Lord stirred up the spirit of Cyrus king of Persia, that he made a proclamation throughout all his kingdom, and put it also in writing, saying, Thus saith Cyrus king of Persia. The Lord God of heaven hath given me all the kingdoms of the earth: and he hath charged me to build him an house at Jerusalem, which is in Judah. Who is there among you of all his people? his God be with him, and let him go up to Jerusalem, which is in Judah, and build the house of the Lord God of Israel (he is the God,) which is in Jerusalem. And whosoever remaineth in any place where he sojourneth, let the men of his place help him with silver, and with gold, and with goods, and with beasts, beside the freewill offering for the house of God that is in Jerusalem"* (Ezra 1:1-4).

Zerubbabel and Joshua began to build the house of God with the help of God's prophets Haggai and Zechariah — *"Then the prophets, Haggai the prophet, and Zechariah the son of Iddo, prophesied unto the Jews that were in Judah and Jerusalem in the name of the God of Israel, even unto them. Then rose up Zerubbabel the son of Shealtiel, and Jeshua the son of Jozadak, and began to build the house of God which is at Jerusalem: and with them were the prophets of God helping them"* (Ezra 5:1-2).

Jesus cleanses the Temple early in His ministry (after the wedding at Cana) — *"And the Jews' passover was at hand, and Jesus went up to Jerusalem, And found in the temple those that sold oxen and sheep and doves, and the changers of money sitting: And when he had made a scourge of small cords, he drove them all out of the temple, and the sheep, and the oxen; and poured out the changers' money, and overthrew the tables; And said unto them that sold doves, Take these things hence; make not my Father's house an house of merchandise"* (John 2:13-16).

Jesus enters Jerusalem as a king on a colt. Zechariah's prophecy (Zech. 9:9) is fulfilled — *"And when he was come into Jerusalem, all the city was moved, saying, Who is this?"* (Matt. 21:10).

Jesus weeps over Jerusalem and predicts its destruction — *"And when he was come near, he beheld the city, and wept over it. Saying, If thou hadst known, even thou, at least in this thy day, the things which belong unto thy peace! but now they are hid from thine eyes. For the days shall come upon thee, that thine enemies shall cast a trench about thee, and compass thee around, and keep thee in on every side. And shall lay thee even with the ground, and thy children within thee; and they shall not leave in thee one stone upon another; because thou knewest not the time of thy visitation"* (Luke 19:41-44).

Paul is taken from the Temple in Jerusalem by an angry mob, then arrested. This event begins his journey to Rome and his Roman imprisonment — *"And all the city was moved, and the people ran together: and they took Paul, and drew him out of the temple: and forthwith the doors were shut. And as they went about to kill him, tidings came unto the chief captain of the band, that all Jerusalem was in an uproar. Who immediately took soldiers and centurions, and ran down unto them: and when they saw the chief captain and the soldiers, they left beating of Paul. Then the chief captain came near, and took him, and commanded him to be bound with two chains; and demanded who he was, and what he had done. And some cried one thing, some another, among the multitude: and when he could not know the certainty for the tumult, he commanded him to be carried into the castle. And when he came upon the stairs, so it was, that he was borne of the soldiers for the violence of the people. For the multitude of the people followed after, crying, Away with him"* (Acts 21:30-36).

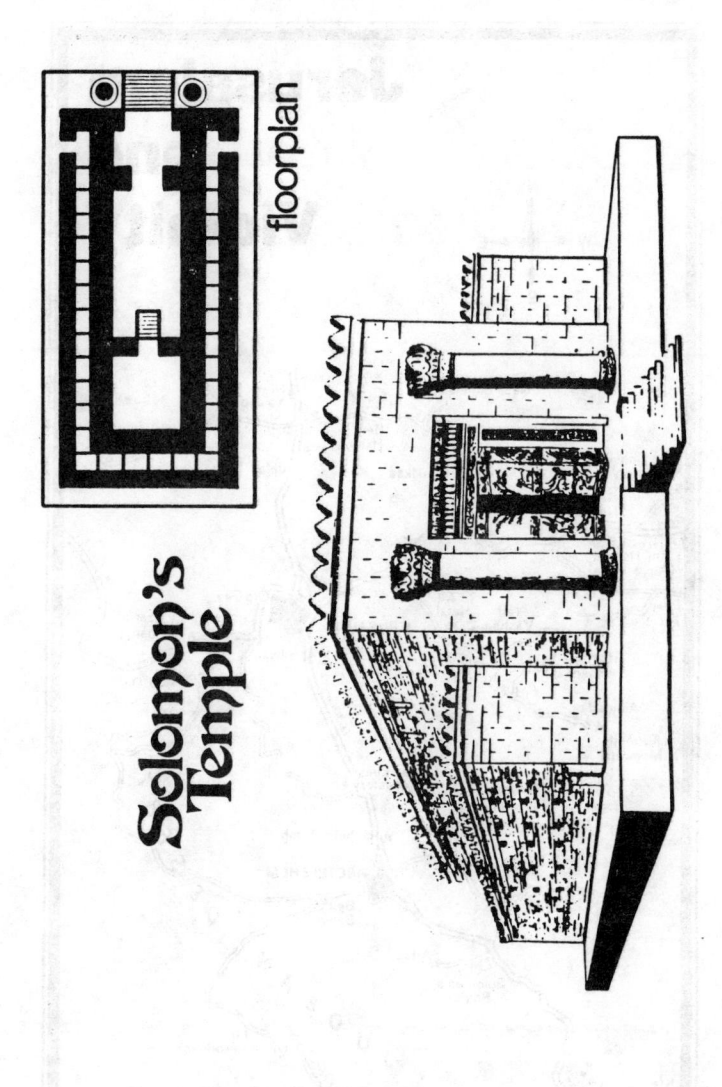

Jerusalem — 105

Solomon's Temple

floorplan

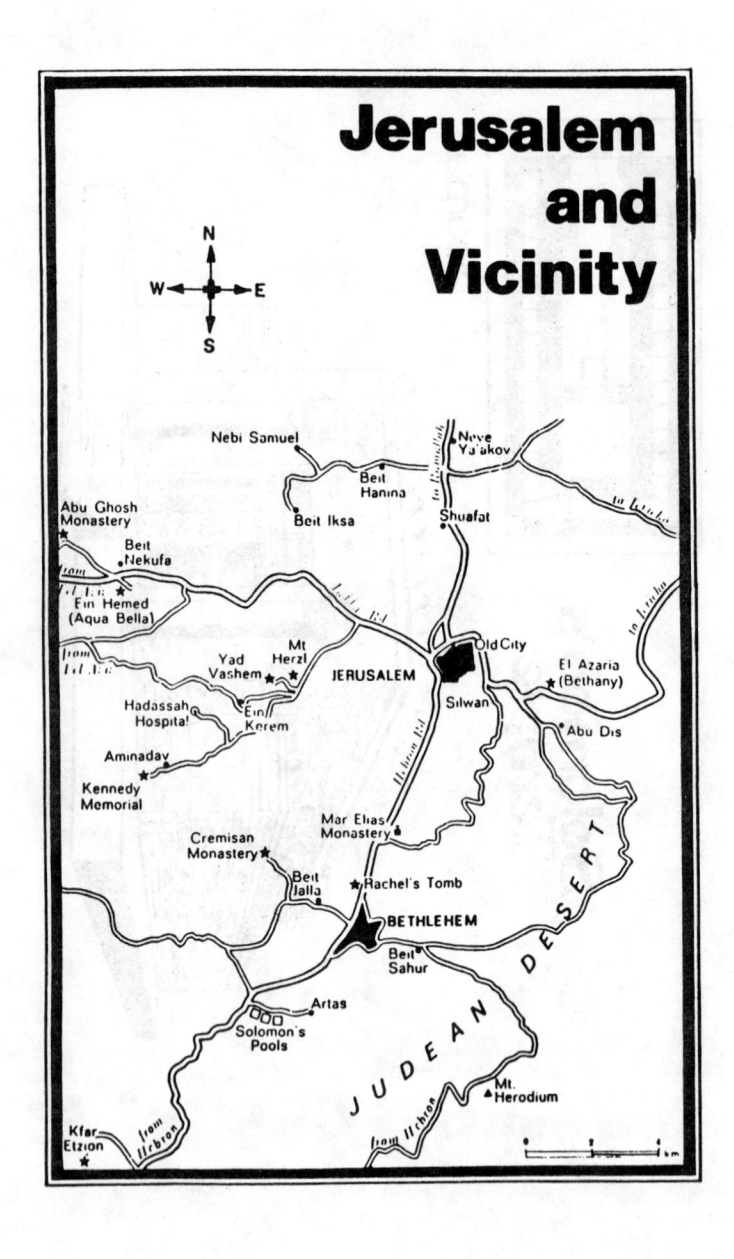

Jerusalem and Vicinity

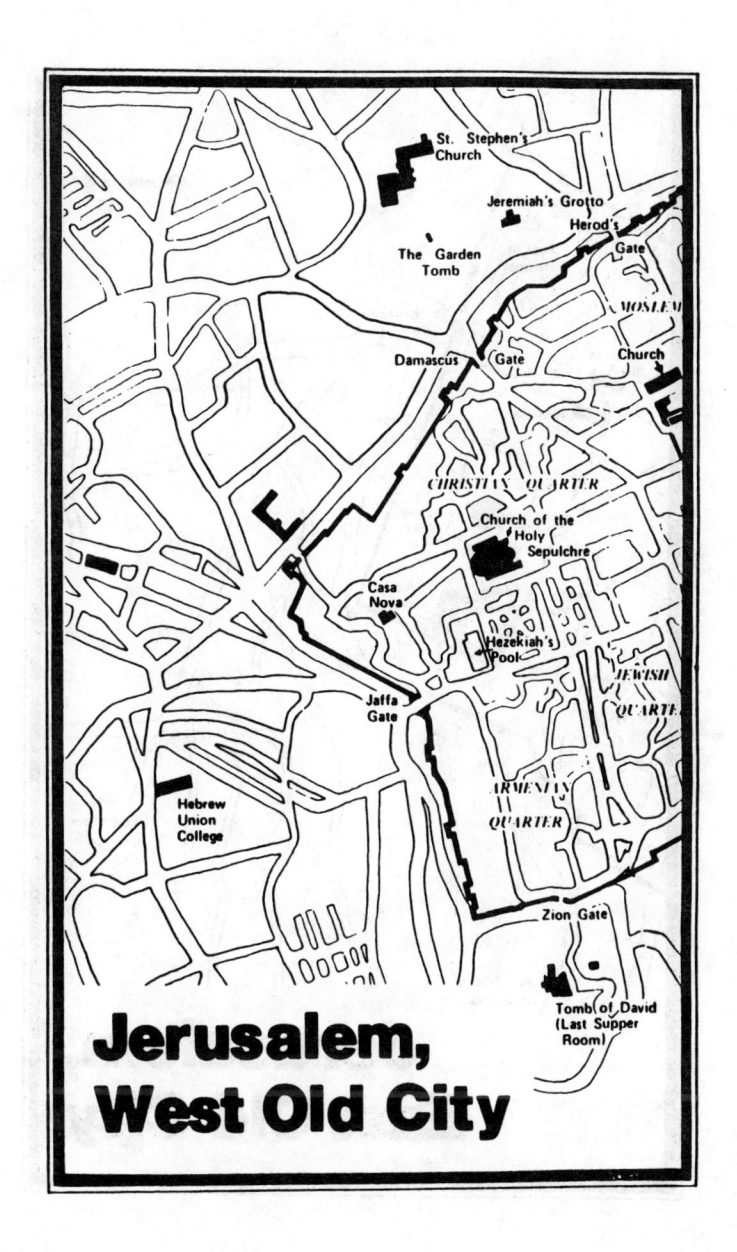

Jerusalem, West Old City

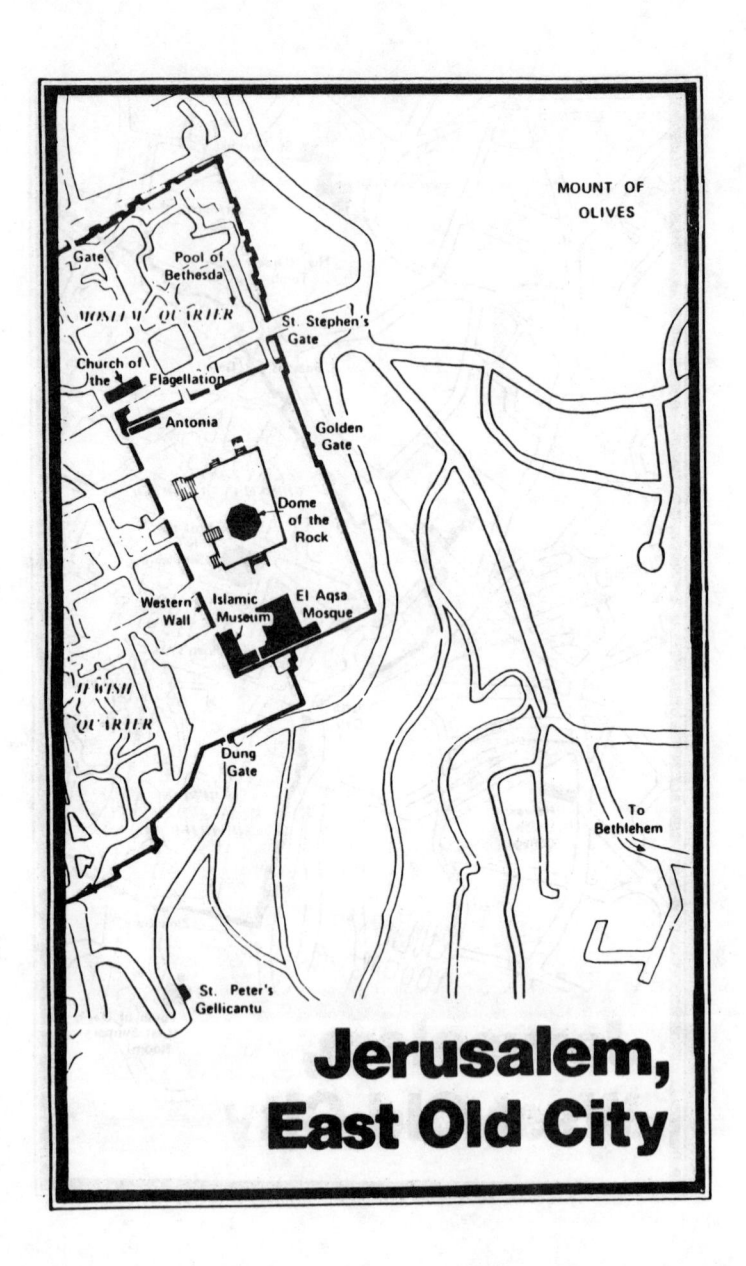

Jerusalem, East Old City

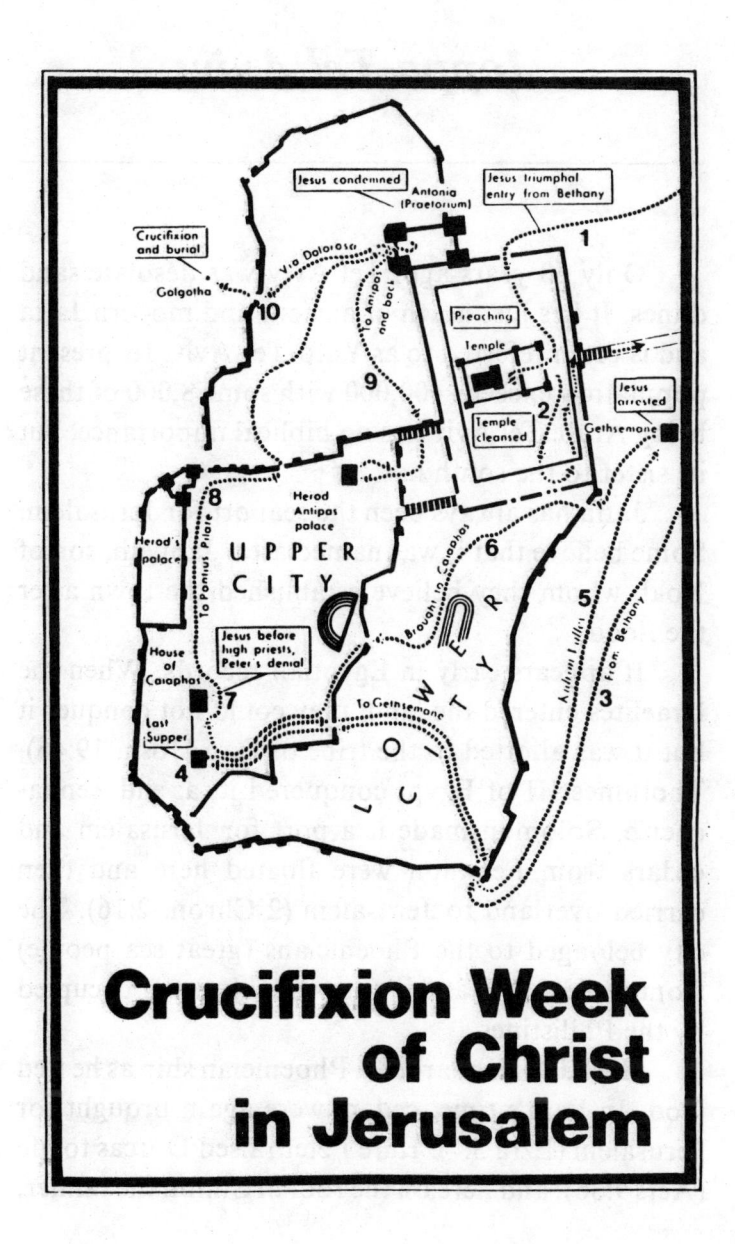

Jerusalem — 109

Crucifixion Week of Christ in Jerusalem

Joppa-Tel Aviv

Only 60 years ago, Tel Aviv was desolate sand dunes. It lies just north of ancient and modern Jaffa and is often referred to as Yofo-Tel-Aviv. Its present population exceeds 400,000 with some 8,000 of these being Arab. Tel Aviv has no biblical importance, but its sister to the south has.

Jaffa has always been the seaport for Jerusalem. Some believe that it was named after Japheth, son of Noah whom they believe established the town after the flood.

It appears early in Egyptian records. When the Israelites entered the land, they could not conquer it but it was allotted to the tribe of Dan (Josh. 19:46). Thothmes III of Egypt conquered it, as did Sennacherib. Solomon made it a port for Jerusalem and cedars from Lebanon were floated here and then carried overland to Jerusalem (2 Chron. 2:16). The city belonged to the Phoenicians (great sea people) from earliest days and it was probably never occupied by the Philistines.

Here Jonah boarded a Phoenician ship as he fled God. In Ezra's time, cedars were again brought for Jerusalem (Ezra 3:7). Here Peter raised Dorcas to life (Acts 9:36), and here on the roof of Simon the tanner,

Peter had his vision and was then sent to witness to Cornelius in Caesarea (Acts 10 and 11). During the Jewish rebellion in A.D. 70 the Jews here hid in the ships in the port, but a violent storm tore the ships apart and most were drowned; those swimming to shore died by the Roman sword.

Biblical References

Solomon made a trade with Hiram for Tyre to furnish cedar logs for the Temple at Jerusalem. It was to this seaport city of Joppa the logs were brought after having been floated down the coast of the Mediterranean Sea. From here they were hauled up to Jerusalem — *"And we will cut wood out of Lebanon, as much as thou shalt need: and we will bring it to thee in floats by sea to Joppa; and thou shalt carry it up to Jerusalem"* (2 Chron. 2:16).

It was at Joppa that Jonah took a ship for Tarshish, fleeing God's call to preach in Nineveh — *"But Jonah rose up to flee unto Tarshish from the presence of the Lord, and went down to Joppa; and he found a ship going to Tarshish: so he paid the fare thereof, and went down into it, to go with them unto Tarshish from the presence of the Lord"* (Jonah 1:3).

Joppa was the home of that wonderful woman who was full of good works — Dorcas — *"Now there was at Joppa a certain disciple named Tabitha, which by* interpretation is called Dorcas: this woman was full of good works and almsdeeds which she did"* (Acts 9:36).

It was here that Peter prayed, and Dorcas was raised from the dead — *"And it came to pass in those days that she was sick, and died: whom when they had washed, they laid her in an upper chamber. But Peter put them all forth, and kneeled down, and prayed; and turning him to the body said, Tabitha, arise. And she opened her eyes: and when she saw Peter, she sat up"* (Acts 9:37, 40).

It was here at Simon the Tanner's house that Peter had the vision of the great sheet being let down from Heaven — *"On the morrow, as they went on their journey, and drew nigh unto the city, Peter went upon the house top to pray about the sixth hour: And he became very hungry, and would have eaten: but while they made ready, he fell into a trance, And saw heaven opened, and a certain vessel descending unto him, as it had been a great sheet knit at the four corners, and let down to the earth: Wherein were all manner of fourfooted beasts of the earth, and wild beasts, and creeping things, and fowls of the air. And there came a voice to him, Rise, Peter, kill, and eat"* (Acts 10:9-13).

Masada

The history of Masada comes by way of Strabo, Pliny, and Josephus in his *Antiquities of the Jews*. Masada appears in the history of Judea in 42 B.C. in connection with the struggle of the house of Antipater and his opponents. After the assassination of Antipater, father of Herod, the brother of the murderer of Antipater (who had in turn been killed by Herod), seized a good many fortresses including Masada, the strongest of all. Herod took Masada from him and released him under truce.

In 40 B.C. Herod fled to Masada with his mother and sister, his betrothed Marianne and her mother, and his younger brother Joseph, after Jerusalem had fallen into the hands of the Parthians, who crowned Mathithyah Antigonus king.

On the way to Masada (after fighting the Jews who pursued him) Herod dismissed 9,000 of his followers, as the place was too small to hold all. Josephus in *Antiquities* says that he kept all who were lightly armed, but they were the strongest. He then left at Masada a garrison of 800 to protect the women and supplies and he went on to Petra.

Antigonus and his army blockaded Joseph at Masada in the winter of 40-39 B.C. and on into the spring. The besieged suffered little, only from the need of more water. But this became so very serious that Joseph planned a flight with 200 soldiers to the Nabateans across the Dead Sea. However, a providential rain fell in the night and filled the cisterns. The relief encouraged them so much that they even set up open attacks against the besiegers and sometimes planned ambushes.

From this period we learn this of Masada:

1. Masada was even then one of the strongest fortresses in all the land by its natural location.
2. Masada had several secret exits.
3. Cisterns were small and they did not suffice for 1,000 persons, even in the winter.
4. Masada would not accommodate over 1,000 persons because of its lack of general facilities.

Herod studied the advantages of Masada and decided to exploit them and make the fortress even stronger. Various constructions were begun. It was furnished as a refuge for Herod, who suspected danger from the Jews, and from Cleopatra, Queen of Egypt. The fortress may be dated 37-31 B.C. during Herod's greatest danger from Cleopatra's domination of Mark Antony. Palaces were added later, when Herod's rule had become more established.

Herod's works included building a casemate wall around the whole area of rock (total of 3,900 feet) of white stone, 18 feet high and 12 feet wide, with 37 towers, each 75 feet high, from which access could be had to the rooms in the thickness of the wall. Most of the interior of the fortress could be cultivated, which gave the variety to the foods served there. Herod built a palace below the walls to the north incline of rock. From the lesson of the seige of 40-39 B.C. Herod took great care to assure an adequate water supply for the garrison. He ordered cutting of cisterns in the rock at each spot used for habitation on the summit and about the palace. He procured enough water as if there were many springs in the area.

Herod built storehouses supplying great quantities of wheat sufficient for years, and plenty of oil, wine, and dates. He brought enough weapons for an army of 10,000 men together with ingots of iron, brass, and lead. He secured approaches to the fortress from the west by building a big tower 1,500 feet from the summit of the fortress. All was completed about 30 B.C. when Herod, with his head in danger, left to meet Caesar Augustus at Rhodes after the battle of Actium. To insure family security in his absence, he sent his mother to Cyprus and his sister and the rest of his family to Masada.

After Herod's death, Masada was held for his son Archelaus and after the disposition of the latter, it was manned by a Roman garrison which remained in possession of it from A.D. 6-66 except for the yeasr of A.D. 41-44 when Agrippa I reigned over Judea. It was during this Roman occupation that Josephus saw Masada during his stay with the Essene sectarian near the Dead Sea (Qumran).

In the first days of the Roman war, a group of zealots took Masada by strategem and the Roman garrison was put to the sword and replaced by a garrison of their own. This was their first success and it strengthened their hands for the Jerusalem struggle. The leader, Menahem, son of Judah and the Galilean, took his close friends there, broke open the royal storehouse, and armed his fellow townsmen and other "brigands." After his death at the hands of Jewish rivals, some of his followers succeeded in escaping to Masada. Among them was Eliezar, son of Yair of Judah, Menahem's nephew, who became the "tyrant of Masada."

The zealots were the undisputed possessors of Masada for the years of the Roman war, A.D. 66-73. Their garrison raided the Idumean villages near them. They raided Engedi on the Passover night and took all the harvest. Because of acts like this, their number increased each day. The fortress served as a point of concentration for those of the *sicari* (a name given to the Jewish zealots who fought the Romans), who were hard-pressed elsewhere. In the last year of the war, the Jewish area was reduced to only 3 fortresses (Herodium, Machrerus in Trans-Jordan, and Masada, which was destined to be the last to fall).

In A.D. 72, two years after the capital had fallen to Roman hands, the Roman governor Flavius Silva marched against Masada at the head of his tenth legion, its auxiliary troops, and 10,000 Jews who were prisoners of war and served as water drawers, hewers of wood, and builders.

The fighters fortified themselves on the height of the mount under the command of Eliezer. The fortress was so impregnable that the Romans never overcame its fortification. At the end of 3 years of the siege, the defenders put themselves to death rather than fall into enemy hands. The fall of Masada in A.D. 73 marked the end of Jewish independence, not to come again until the year 1948.

Josephus, in his *Wars of the Jews*, describes the heroic end of Masada.

"They then chose ten men by lot out of them to slay all the rest, every one of whom lay himself down by his wife and children on the ground, and threw his arms about them, and they offered their necks to the stroke of those who by lot executed that melancholy office: and when these ten had, without fear slain them all, they made the same rule of casting lots for themselves, that he whose lot should be first kill the other nine, and all, kill himself. . . . So these people died with this intention, that they would leave not so much as one soul among them all alive to be subject to the Romans. . . . The dead were nine hundred and sixty in number.

"And the Romans came within the palace and met with the multitude of the slain, but could take no pleasure in the fact, though it were done

to their enemies. Nor could they do other than wonder at the courage of their resolution and the immovable contempt of death, which so great a number as them had shown, when they went through with such an action as that was."

Metsuda — "stronghold" is the name of the fortress of the mount. The Hebrew name has been Hellenized into Masada and thus it appears in ancient literature. Some scholars surmise that this site is already referred to in the episode of David's flight from Saul the king. In 1 Chronicles 12:8 it says of David's men:

". . . into the hold [metsuda] *to the wilderness men of might, and men of war fit for the battle, that could handle shield and buckler, whose faces were like the faces of lions, and were as swift as the roes upon the mountains."*

Jesus prophesied the fall of Jerusalem and said that in those days the people of Judea would flee into the mountains (Mark 13:14; Luke 21:21).

Masada — 119

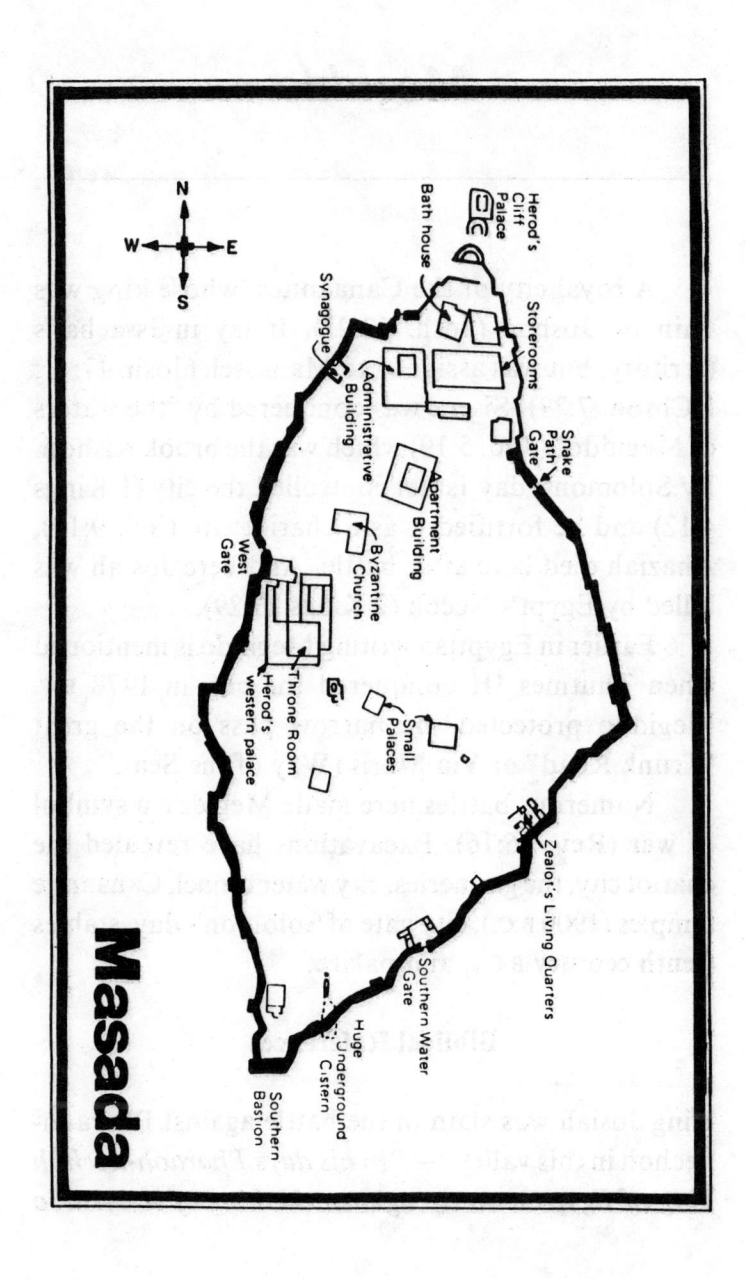

Masada

- Herod's Cliff Palace
- Bath house
- Storerooms
- Snake Path Gate
- Synagogue
- Administrative Building
- Apartment Building
- Byzantine Church
- West Gate
- Herod's western palace
- Throne Room
- Small Palaces
- Zealot's Living Quarters
- Southern Water Gate
- Huge Underground Cistern
- Southern Bastion

Megiddo

A royal city of the Canaanites, whose king was slain by Joshua (Josh. 12:21). It lay in Issachar's territory, but was assigned to Manasseh (Josh. 17:11; 1 Chron. 7:29). Sisera was conquered by "the waters of Megiddo" (Jud. 5:19) which was the brook Kishon. By Solomon's day Israel controlled the city (1 Kings 4:12) and he fortified it as a chariot city (Sol. 9:15). Ahaziah died here after battle. And here Josiah was killed by Egypt's Necoh (2 Kings 23:29).

Earlier in Egyptian writing Megiddo is mentioned when Thutmes III conquered the city in 1478 B.C. Megiddo protected the narrow pass on the great "Trunk Road" or Via Maris (Way of the Sea).

Numerous battles here made Megiddo a symbol of war (Rev. 16:16). Excavations have revealed the chariot city, the graineries, city water tunnel, Canaanite temples (1900 B.C.), city gate of Solomon's day, stables (tenth century B.C.), and palace.

Biblical References

King Josiah was slain in the battle against Pharaoh-nechoh in this valley — *"In his days Pharaoh-nechoh king of Egypt went up against the king of Assyria to the river Euphrates: and king Josiah went against him; and he slew him at Megiddo, when he had seen him. And his servants carried him in a chariot dead from Megiddo, and brought him to Jerusalem, and buried him in his own sepulchre"* (2 Kings 23:29-30).

Megiddo was the scene of decisive battles so often that it became a symbol of war and of great mourning — *"In that day there shall be a great mourning in Jerusalem, as the mourning of Hadadrimmon in the valley of Megiddo"* (Zech. 12:11).

The final rebellion against God, Armageddon, will be fought in the Valley of Megiddo — *And I saw three unclean spirits like frogs come out of the mouth of the dragon, and out of the mouth of the beast, and out of the mouth of the false prophet. For they are the spirits of devils, working miracles, which go forth unto the kings of the earth and of the whole world, to gather them to the battle of that great day of God Almighty. Behold, I come as a thief, Blessed is he that watcheth, and keepeth his garments, lest he walk naked, and they see his shame. And he gathered them together into a place called in the Hebrew tongue Armageddon"* (Rev. 16:13-16).

Nazareth

The home of Joseph and Mary, and for 30 years the scene of Jesus' early life (Matt. 2:23; Mark 1:9, 26-32; Luke 2:39, 51; 4:16). Thus, He was called Jesus the Nazarene (though born in Bethlehem). Even His later disciples were called Nazarenes (yet none were from Nazareth).

Lying 75 miles north of Jerusalem, the town doesn't appear in the Old Testament, yet due to the location and water supply the city was probably occupied as early as 1200 B.C. It was built on white limestone and in a basin of Senomian chalk, yet it is 1230 feet above sea level. The village grew around the spring today called the "Well of the Virgin." It was very small in Jesus' day, but today is the largest city in the district. When Jesus lived there the largest city of the area was Sepphoris (capital of Galilee, a few miles to the north).

The Nazareth basin is nestled in the lower hills of Galilee just before they sink into the Plain of Esdraelon. It lies midway between the Sea of Galilee and the Mediterranean Sea.

Here Jesus grew to manhood, knowing well the street markets, carpenter's shops, fields, and synagogue. Later, after preaching his first recorded sermon, the villagers sought to destroy Him. He did not do many mighty works there because of their unbelief (Matt. 13:58). From here Jesus could have viewed Jezreel as a child and recalled Israel's history. To the west lay Mt. Carmel (Elijah and the Baal prophets), to the south was Megiddo, to the southeast lay Mt. Gilboa (where Jonathan and Saul were killed) and also Mt. Tabor (where Deborah and Barak assembled against Sisera.

Biblical References

Gabriel visits Mary in Nazareth to announce the coming birth of Jesus — *"And in the sixth month the angel Gabriel was sent from God unto a city of Galilee, named Nazareth, To a virgin espoused to a man whose name was Joseph, of the house of David; and the virgin's name was Mary. And the angel came in unto her, and said, Hail, thou that art highly favoured, the Lord is with thee: blessed art thou among women . . . And, behold, thou shalt conceive in thy womb, and bring forth a son, and shalt call his name Jesus . . . And the angel departed from her"* (Luke 1:26-38).

After their sojourn in Egypt to escape the wrath of Herod, Mary and Joseph brought Jesus back to Nazareth to live and grow to manhood — *"But when Herod was dead, behold an angel of the Lord appeared in a dream to Joseph in Egypt, Saying, Arise, and take the young child and his mother, and go into the land of Israel: for they are dead which sought the young child's life . . . And he came and dwelt in a city called Nazareth . . .* " (Matt. 2:19-23).

Jesus was baptized in the Jordan River as He was leaving Nazareth — *"And it came to pass in those days, that Jesus came from Nazareth of Galilee, and was baptized of John in Jordan"* (Mark 1:9).

Christ identified Himself as Jesus of Nazareth when He met Saul on the road to Damascus — *"And I answered, Who art thou, Lord? And he said unto me, I am Jesus of Nazareth, whom thou persecutest"* (Acts 22:8).

Samaria

King Omri of Israel moved his capital here in 880 B.C. and built a metropolis there (1 Kings 16:24). It became the residence and burial place for the kings of Israel (1 Kings 16:28; 22:37; 2 Kings 10:35; 13:9, 13; 14:16). It lay in Ephraim and rises 300 feet above the plains below. The sides are steep and easily defended. To seek to destroy the city was to court disaster. Enemies could only rely on famine in the city (2 Kings 6:24). Truly Omri made an excellent choice for a capital. A city wall is traced the entire circle of the mount. Here is found Omri's palace, as well as Ahab's, and later Herod's.

Under Jezebel it became a center of idol worship to Baal and Ashteroth (1 Kings 16:32). Jehoram later put away the pillar (2 Kings 3:2). Still later Jehu put an end to the instruments of idolatry (2 Kings 10:19). In the area near a pool the dogs lapped Ahab's blood from his chariot. Isaiah, Jeremiah, Ezekiel, Hosea, Amos, and Micah all refer to the idolatry of Samaria.

Ben-Hadad II beseiged the city but was defeated (1 Kings 20:1-21). Syrian attempts to conquer the city during Jehoram's reign were frustrated by Elisha (2 Kings 6:8). Later Ben-Hadad almost took the city (2 Kings 6:24), but a mysterious panic seized the Syrian army and they deserted their camp. The incident was reported by lepers outside the city (2 Kings 7). Here 70 sons of Ahab were slain by Jehu (2 Kings 10:1). Here Ahaziah was also slain (2 Kings 9:27). Shalmaneser started the final seige of Samaria under King Hoshea's reign and the city fell to Sargon II after 3 years in 772 B.C. (2 Kings 17:5; 18:9), closing the era of the Northern Kingdom. The people were deported and colonists were brought in to populate the area (2 Kings 17:24).

Alexander the Great took the city in 331 B.C. replacing the citizens with Syro-Macedonian people. The city suffered attacks under the Ptolemy powers and fell to John Hyrcanus in 120 B.C., who destroyed it completely. Pompey rebuilt the city and Herod gave it renewed splendor calling it Sebaste (in honor of Emperor Augusta). A temple was dedicated to Caesar. Here Herod killed the only human he probably ever loved, his wife Marianne, and soon after slaughtered his sons with his own hand. Philip probably preached here (Acts 8).